MAX notes®

Toni Morrison's

The Bluest Eye, A Novel

Text by
Christopher A. Hubert
(B.A., Bates College)
Department of English
Oryol Pedagogical University
Oryol, Russia

Illu...
Jerd...

Research & Education Association
Dr. M. Fogiel, Director

MAXnotes® for
THE BLUEST EYE, A NOVEL

Printed in the United States of America

Library of Congress Control Number 2001089030

International Standard Book Number 0-87891-008-5

MAXnotes® is a registered trademark of
Research & Education Association, Piscataway, New Jersey 08854

What **MAXnotes**® *Will Do for You*

This book is intended to help you absorb the essential contents and features of Toni Morrison's *The Bluest Eye, A Novel* and to help you gain a thorough understanding of the work. Our book has been designed to do this more quickly and effectively than any other study guide.

For best results, this **MAXnotes** book should be used as a companion to the actual work, not instead of it. The interaction between the two will greatly benefit you.

To help you in your studies, this book presents the most up-to-date interpretations of every section of the actual work, followed by questions and fully explained answers that will enable you to analyze the material critically. The questions also will help you to test your understanding of the work and will prepare you for discussions and exams.

Meaningful illustrations are included to further enhance your understanding and enjoyment of the literary work. The illustrations are designed to place you into the mood and spirit of the work's settings.

The **MAXnotes** also include summaries, character lists, explanations of plot, and section-by-section analyses. A biography of the author and discussion of the work's historical context will help you put this literary piece into the proper framework of what is taking place.

The use of this study guide will save you the hours of preparation time that would ordinarily be required to arrive at a complete grasp of this work of literature. You will be well prepared for classroom discussions, homework, and exams. The guidelines that are included for writing papers and reports on various topics will prepare you for any added work which may be assigned.

The **MAXnotes** will take your grades "to the max."

Dr. Max Fogiel
Program Director

Contents

Each Book includes List of Characters, Summary, Analysis, Study Questions and Answers, and Suggested Essay Topics.

MAXnotes® are simply the best – but don't just take our word for it...

"... I have told every bookstore in the area to carry your MAXnotes. They are the only notes I recommend to my students. There is no comparison between MAXnotes and all other notes ..."
— *High School Teacher & Reading Specialist, Arlington High School, Arlington, MA*

"... I discovered the MAXnotes when a friend loaned me her copy of the *MAXnotes for Romeo and Juliet*. The book really helped me understand the story. Please send me a list of stores in my area that carry the MAXnotes. I would like to use more of them ..."
— *Student, San Marino, CA*

"... The two MAXnotes titles that I have used have been very, very useful in helping me understand the subject matter reviewed. Thank you for creating the MAXnotes series ..."
— *Student, Morrisville, PA*

A Glance at Some of the Characters

Claudia

Frieda

MacTeers

Pecola

Pauline

Cholly

Maureen

Soaphead

SECTION ONE

Introduction

The Life and Work of Toni Morrison

Toni Morrison was born Chloe Anthony Wofford on February 18, 1931. Her birthplace was Lorain, Ohio, which also serves as the setting for *The Bluest Eye*. Her parents both moved to Lorain from the South in search of better living conditions. Young Chloe was influenced greatly by her parents and their never-ending quest to improve the lives of their children. The small community was also very supportive of others and, although she was a shy girl, she remembers fondly the support she received as a youngster.

Toni was an excellent student, with a particular fondness for literature. She graduated from Howard University in 1953 with a bachelor's degree in English and received a master's degree from Cornell University two years later. At Howard, she changed her name to Toni and was an active participant in their drama club. She continued to love literature, however, and after receiving her master's degree, she taught literature at Texas Southern University briefly before returning to Howard.

It was at Howard University that she met Harold Morrison, an architect, whom she later married. The Morrisons had two sons together but divorced in 1965. Morrison then relocated to Syracuse, where she became an editor for Random House. By 1967 she was a senior editor, but still desired some sort of release for her creative energy.

She was active in writers' support groups while at Howard but still had not published any works. In Syracuse, she decided to rewrite a short story she had written at Howard about "a girl who wanted blue eyes." She was encouraged by a fellow editor, Alan Rancler, to turn this story into a full-length novel. *The Bluest Eye* was turned down by a few publishing companies before being printed by Holt, Rhinehart, and Winston in 1970. The book was given favorable reviews and established her as a talented new writer with a gift for language. A second novel, *Sula*, was published in 1973 and received a nomination for the National Book Award.

It was her third novel, *Song of Solomon*, that catapulted her to national prominence. Published in 1977, this novel also won the National Book Critics Circle Award. Her most famous novel is undoubtedly 1987's *Beloved*, which won the Pulitzer Prize. *The Bluest Eye*, as well as Morrison's other novels, have been studied in schools around the country. In addition to writing, Morrison has produced a play, taught and lectured at Yale, Berkeley, and Princeton, and edited anthologies and critical studies of African-American literature. In 1993, she won the Nobel Prize for Literature, becoming the first African-American woman to do so. Further information about Toni Morrison can also be found in the MAXnotes® literary digests for *Beloved*, *Jazz*, and *Song of Solomon*.

Historical Background

The Bluest Eye is set in a steel mill town in the 1940s. During the Great Depression, many people migrated in search of jobs, and the characters of the novel, much like Toni Morrison's family, come to Lorain in search of better lives and better jobs. However, economic recovery did not come to America until the start of World War II, and life in these towns was wracked with poverty and squalor.

A prominent theme in the novel is the idea of beauty and its standards. One of the most famous child actresses at the time was Shirley Temple, whose movies in the 1930s and 40s were immensely popular. Most of her films were family pictures, slight in plot and optimistic in tone, made with the intention of uplifting the spirits of those who were suffering through the depression (one of her films was entitled *The Little Princess*). Other actresses mentioned are Greta Garbo, Ginger Rogers, and Hedy Lamarr, all white women who epitomized the standards of beauty at the time.

Black actors and actresses in movies of this era usually portrayed waiters or maids and were chiefly employed as comic relief.

Although their choices of roles were limited, a few black actors and actresses managed to gain fame and stardom. Hattie McDaniel won the Academy Award for Best Supporting Actress in the 1939 film *Gone With the Wind*, becoming the first black person to do so. As these actors gained prominence, they attempted to protest the lack of quality roles for blacks, but could do practically nothing to change the rigid stereotyping of Hollywood. Some independent production companies, such as Toddy Pictures, managed to release a few films featuring all-black casts that were designed for black audiences. These films were usually inexpensive to make, because of the lack of financing available, and designed to provide light entertainment rather than commentary on social issues. During an era when Franklin Roosevelt integrated the armed forces and government offices, the film industry definitely was not progressive in terms of civil rights.

Master List of Characters

Claudia MacTeer—*A young black girl who lives in an old house in Lorain; fiercely independent and resents the adults who give her orders; has an uncontrollable hatred for the white dolls that she receives for Christmas.*

Frieda MacTeer—*Claudia's older sister; protective of Claudia but is more good-natured; considers herself to be wiser than Claudia but still acts like a little girl in many situations.*

Mr. and Mrs. MacTeer—*Claudia and Frieda's parents; They are harsh to their children at times but are fiercely protective of them.*

Pecola Breedlove—*An ugly twelve-year-old girl who wants blue eyes more than anything else in the world; constantly teased by children at school and abused by her parents; believes that the world will treat her differently once she is beautiful.*

Cholly Breedlove—*Pecola's father; a man who is constantly drunk and fighting with his wife Pauline.*

Pauline (Mrs.) Breedlove—*Pecola's mother; a woman who is a live-in maid with a white family and seems more concerned with her employer's family growth and progress than the health of her own family; stays with Cholly in order to chastise him for his drinking.*

Sammy Breedlove—*Pecola's older brother; a boy who either is running away from home or fighting with others.*

Poland, China, and Miss Marie (the Maginot Line)—*Three prostitutes who occupy the apartment above the Breedloves' place; Pecola visits them often, and they treat her well.*

Mr. Yacobowski—*Owner of a local grocery store.*

Mr. Henry Washington—*A middle-aged man who rents a room from the MacTeers for a brief period of time; kicked out of the house by Mr. MacTeer after he molests Frieda.*

Maureen Peal—*A light-skinned black girl who quickly becomes the most popular girl in school; the other students want to be her friend because they think she is beautiful. She befriends Pecola for a short time before turning on her.*

Geraldine—*A light-skinned lady who devotes herself to removing all the passion from her life in exchange for security in marriage; harbors a bitter resentment towards dark-skinned blacks and forces her son to stay away from other black boys.*

Louis Junior—*Geraldine's son; hates his mother and the cat that is the object of his mother's affections; plays a cruel trick on Pecola and attacks the cat in the process.*

Soaphead Church—*A man who analyzes dreams and promises to fix family problems; tricks Pecola into believing she has blue eyes.*

Rosemary Villanucci—*A rich girl who lives next door to Claudia and Frieda; teases the MacTeer girls often from the window of her father's car.*

Aunt Jimmy—*The aunt of Cholly Breedlove's mother, who had abandoned Cholly right after he was born; raises Cholly herself rather than return him to his natural mother.*

Blue Jack—*An old man who worked at the feed store with Cholly Breedlove; used to entertain Cholly with stories.*

M'Dear—*A respected midwife who also prescribed home remedies for the ladies of the town in which Cholly Breedlove grew up.*

O. V.—*Aunt Jimmy's brother.*

Jake—*An older cousin who tries to pick up girls with Cholly Breedlove.*

Darlene—*Cholly Breedlove's first girlfriend.*

Samson Fuller—*Cholly's natural father.*

Bay Boy, Woodrow Cain, Buddy Wilson, and Junie Bug—*Four boys who tease Pecola in the playground.*

Ada and Fowler Williams—*Pauline Breedlove's parents.*

Chicken and Pie Williams—*Pauline's younger twin brothers.*

Ivy—*A singer in Pauline's childhood church.*

The Fishers—*The white family that hires Mrs. Breedlove as a maid; The father works as a real estate agent.*

The Fishers' daughter— *Mr. and Mrs. Fisher's adorable little daughter.*

Velma—*Soaphead Church's ex-wife.*

Summary of the Novel

Claudia MacTeer is a young black girl growing up in the small mill town of Lorain, Ohio. Life for her is difficult, because her parents are too busy to show loving compassion. Claudia often finds it necessary to fight for herself, because other children try to put her down while adults are too busy with their own affairs and only notice children when there is work to be done. Claudia finds a lot of her anger and aggression directed towards the little white dolls that she receives as presents. It seems to her that these white dolls are given more love and attention than a flesh-and-blood black child.

The lives of Claudia and her sister Frieda take an interesting turn when Pecola Breedlove is temporarily placed in the MacTeer home by county officials. Pecola's father burnt down their home, and Pecola needs a place to stay while her father serves his jail sentence. Claudia and Frieda like Pecola because she is quiet and shy, and responds to their offers of graham crackers and milk. The milk is brought in a Shirley Temple mug. Pecola and Frieda both love Shirley Temple and soon become involved in a discussion about her. Claudia finds it hard to relate to this topic but nevertheless they enjoy each other's company.

The Breedlove family soon comes together again and finds a different home in an ugly house on the corner of a forgotten street. We learn that the entire Breedlove family has serious problems with self-esteem. The Breedloves go through life believing in their ugliness. Pauline, or Mrs. Breedlove, devotes her time to fighting with her husband Cholly and taking care of a white family. Cholly, when he is not fighting his wife, spends his days drinking. Their children are either abused or neglected, and each child has coped with this abuse or neglect in a special manner. Sammy has already run away from home many times, while Pecola spends her time trying to be invisible. Pecola prays for blue eyes, because she believes that if she were a beautiful girl, everyone in town would treat her nicely.

Pecola, however, is abused by almost everybody in the town. One day, she is brutally teased by a group of boys when she is unexpectedly saved by Frieda, Claudia, and a new girl named Maureen Peal. Maureen Peal is a beautiful light-skinned girl that becomes friendly towards Pecola for a while. However, Maureen soon turns on the other girls, using her own beauty as a weapon against them. Pecola is also the victim of a cruel prank by a light-skinned boy named Louis Junior, who is resentful towards dark-skinned blacks.

The reader is shown how Pecola's parents met each other. Pauline Williams' dreams are dashed at an early age when she steps on a nail and develops a crippled foot. It is only when she meets Cholly Breedlove that she begins to feel the magic of life. However, when the newly married couple move to Lorain, they begin to drift apart from each other. Pauline takes solace in the movies, watching the pretty actresses and emulating their hairstyles, but she becomes uglier and uglier. Once she has two children, she begins to spend most of her days taking care of a white family, so she can at least keep the illusion of being beautiful.

Cholly also had a difficult childhood, having been abandoned by both parents. The only person who takes care of him is his Aunt Jimmy, but she dies while Cholly is still a young boy. At Aunt Jimmy's funeral, Cholly meets another girl and they go off into a nearby field. Their kissing is interrupted by two white hunters, who order Cholly to make love to the girl while they watch. Cholly, shamed and humiliated, transfers this anger to the girl rather than the hunters. Soon after this incident, Cholly travels to Macon, Georgia in search of his natural father. Cholly finds his father but is too afraid to introduce himself and runs away. Without his parents, Cholly lives a life of total freedom but is confused once he has children with Pauline. He is unable to understand how to love his children, and deals with this confusion by drinking. One drunken night, he comes home and finds Pecola washing the dishes. When Pecola scratches her leg with her foot, it causes Cholly to remember when he first met this wife. The memory of tickling his wife's foot, as well as his drunken state, are factors which lead him to rape Pecola.

After the rape, Pecola decides to go to Soaphead Church, the "spiritual advisor" of the town. Pecola asks him for blue eyes, and the man is moved. He decides to help the girl and deceives her into poisoning a dog that he hates, telling her that it would be a sign that God has heard her prayers. Once Pecola leaves, Soaphead Church writes a letter to God, telling Him that he has granted this girl her wish because God has obviously not been listening to her prayers.

Pecola's pregnancy at the hands of her father causes a terrible scandal and Pecola is thrown out of school. The town condemns Cholly but feels that Pecola must share some of the blame for not fighting back. When Claudia and Frieda hear about their friend, they decide to pray for her and sacrifice some flower seeds that they were going to use to make money. However, the seeds that the girls planted refuse to grow, and Pecola's baby dies. Claudia and Frieda avoid Pecola afterwards, thinking that they had failed their friend. Pecola is left to wander the streets. She has been driven insane by the abuse and spends her time looking in a mirror and talking with her imaginary friend about her blue eyes. Claudia, now grown up, looks back at that time and understands that it was not her fault that Pecola had become insane, and it is now too late to help Pecola recover.

Estimated Reading Time

The 160-page novel is short but rather complex. While it is possible to complete the novel in ten hours, it might be necessary to review and reread the entire novel in order to gain a better understanding of Morrison's use of structure. Teachers should probably allow extra class time for discussion, since there are some controversial scenes (such as Cholly's rape of his daughter) that will provoke serious debate among the students.

The Bluest Eye

"Dick and Jane"

Summary

The novel begins with a small passage that is similar in style to the "Dick and Jane" readers that were used for young children. Morrison uses this passage to emphasize the ideal of beauty that children are taught at an early age. The family lives in an idyllic "green-and-white" house, and Jane is wearing a "pretty red dress," which is not the most practical of garments since she "wants to play." The passage in the section is repeated three times, and the words come closer to each other with each repetition until the passage becomes nonsense. Morrison uses this technique to emphasize how lessons are often "drummed" into children at an early age until the lessons become fact. This information, however, is not the same as a mathematics lesson. In this "textbook," a family that bears no connection with reality becomes the standard by which millions of children expect to live.

Analysis

Although the meaning of this opening passage will become clear as the novel is read, there is one notable action in the passage that *foreshadows* the action of the novel. Jane is looking for someone to play with her. Why is it so difficult for Jane to find a companion? The mother "laughs" when she is asked to play, and the father "smiles." The friendly language of the passage masks the fact that no one seems to want to play with Jane, until a "friend" is found at the passage's end. In the perfect world suggested by the textbook, it should be easy for Jane to find a playmate. The long search shows that problems can exist in what seems to be the most perfect of places. Even Jane, in her pretty dress and beautiful house, seems to have trouble finding a friend.

Introduction

Summary

A woman talks about the fall of 1941, a time when none of the marigolds that she had planted along with her sister had blossomed. These flowers were planted when they had discovered that their friend, Pecola, was pregnant with her father's child. In their disappointment, each girl used to blame the other, but now the woman wonders if it was "the earth" that caused the flowers to die. In any case, she knows that "nothing remains except Pecola and the unyielding earth." It is clear to her that it is too late to help her friend, so the only thing left to discuss is why this tragedy occurred in the first place. However, it is too painful for this woman to mention why this happened, so "one must take refuge in *how*."

Analysis

This introduction is primarily used to foreshadow, or give hints to future events in the novel. The reader understands that the events that will follow are tragic, because of the symbol of the marigolds. Whatever happens later in the novel will cause the marigolds to die, and cause the still-unknown narrator to feel pain. The reader also learns that the narrator had blamed herself for the tragedy, but has since come to realize that "nobody's" marigolds had grown that year. This realization has helped the narrator accept the tragic events, although she still is affected by the death of Pecola's baby and "our innocence."

Since "nothing remains but Pecola and the unyielding earth," the narrator feels that no more hurt can come from telling the reader of the events. However, the narrator leaves the discussion of *why* this occurred to the reader, since "*why* is [still] difficult to handle." The narrator is too affected to offer any insight of her own, indicating that the events that follow will shock and affect the reader as well.

AUTUMN
Chapter 1

New Characters:

Claudia: *a nine-year-old girl living in a quiet Southern town*

Frieda: *Claudia's older sister, ten-years-old*

Mr. and Mrs. Mac Teer: *Claudia and Frieda's parents*

Mr. Henry Washington: *a middle-aged man who rents a room from Claudia and Frieda's parents*

Pecola Breedlove: *an eleven-year-old girl who lives with Claudia and Frieda briefly when her father burns down the family home*

Rosemary Villanucci: *a rich girl who lives next door to Claudia and Frieda*

Summary

It is the autumn of 1940. Claudia is nine-years-old and lives in an old house with her parents and her ten-year-old sister, Frieda. She remembers the autumn as a time when two new people come into her house. Mr. Henry Washington moves in as a tenant, and immediately delights the girls with his charm and wit. Pecola Breedlove is placed in the house as a social case when her father is put in jail for burning down their own home. Claudia and Frieda immediately befriend her, because she is quiet and receptive to their offers of milk and snacks. When she is given milk in a Shirley Temple cup, Pecola makes a remark about how beautiful she is, and starts a conversation with Frieda about Shirley Temple. Claudia has always hated little white girls for the attention they received. For birthdays and Christmas, she would tear apart the white dolls that were given to her in an effort "to see what it was that the whole world said was lovable." More often than not, the adults would cry

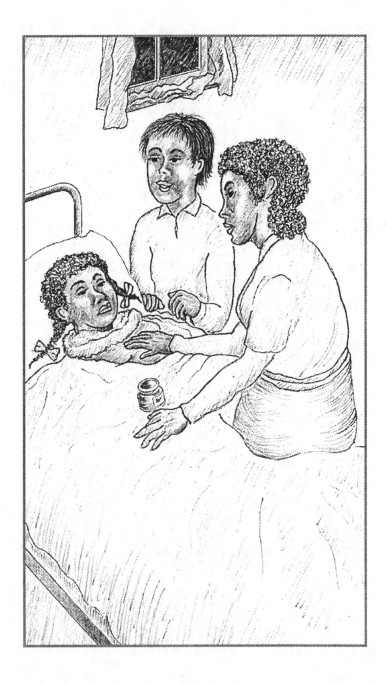

over the dolls that Claudia had destroyed, as if these plastic tokens were actually real.

Pecola drinks three quarts of milk in order to touch the Shirley Temple cup. Claudia and Frieda's mother discovers this and starts to complain, shaming the three girls. While the girls decide where they should go, Pecola starts menstruating. She is scared at first but Frieda calms her down, telling her that "it just means you can have a baby." The girls attempt to clean her off secretly and bury her bloody underpants in the backyard. However, Rosemary Villanucci, a neighboring girl, spots them and calls their mother. Mama, who accuses the girls of being "nasty," whips Frieda and begins to whip Pecola. When she grabs Pecola, she notices the blood and asks the girls what is going on. Claudia finally manages to tell her mother what has happened, and Mama apologizes and takes Pecola up to the bathroom to clean her. That evening, both girls are proud of Pecola, but Pecola stays up wondering what she must do now to have a baby. Frieda whispers that "someone has to love you," and goes to sleep. Pecola still wonders "How?"

Analysis

The one aspect of the novel that is immediately noticed is its tragic tone; the novel seems to be completely devoid of hope. We have already learned at the introduction that a girl will give birth to her father's baby; the reader assumes that she will be raped by her own father. By mentioning this at the start of the novel, Morrison robs any potential celebration of its joy. Pecola's menstruation should be a happy event, because it marks the transition from a girl to a woman. Frieda's happy announcement to Pecola that she can now have a baby is now tragic, given the events that have been foreshadowed by the adult narrator, who the reader now realizes is Claudia.

Morrison uses the setting to establish the unhappy tone of the novel; while "Dick and Jane" live in a pretty green-and-white house, the first scene featuring Claudia and Frieda, features them gathering coal by the railroad tracks. The use of the "Dick and Jane" passage becomes clear; Morrison presents a contrast to the fantasy world that is so often taught to children. The cold reality in which Claudia and Frieda live is so far removed from the world of "Dick

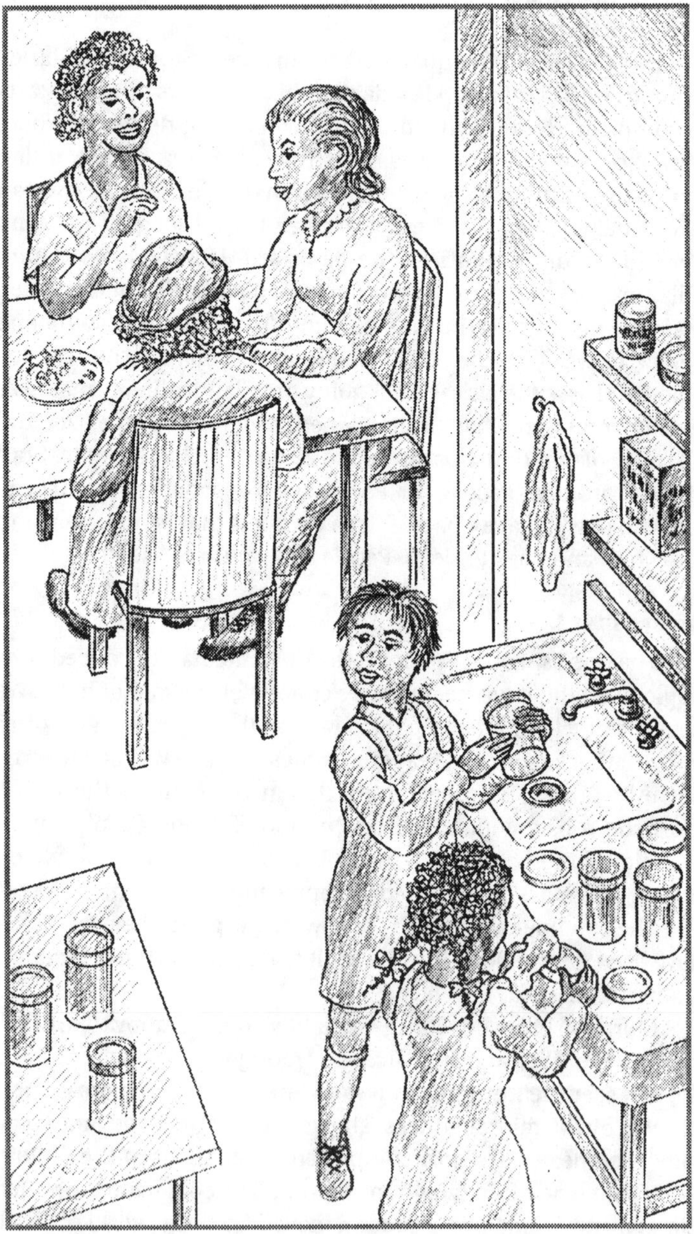

and Jane" that the reader is immediately struck by this seemingly cruel world.

However, love does exist in the real world. This is shown when Claudia falls ill, even though Claudia's parents "shake their heads in disgust at [her] lack of consideration." Their parents simply do not have the time to deal with a sick child; they are too busy trying to earn a living for their children, so "[a child's] illness is treated with contempt." Claudia forgives her parents for their apparent lack of caring. Although she remembers the pain and humiliation when she is scolded for vomiting over her bed, she is able to understand why she is treated this way. When the work is done, and there is some spare time for Claudia's mother, she finally can take the time to worry about her child. Claudia's mother comes in one night and rests her hand on Claudia's forehead. It is this moment that Claudia treasures; through all the suffering, she is able to remember her mother as "somebody with hands who does not want [her] to die."

The characters of Claudia and Pecola are quickly established in their differences. The most striking difference is the world in which each girl chooses to live. Claudia is grounded in reality, and understands that it is sometimes necessary to fight for respect; therefore, she is quick to strike out at real or imagined insults. She attacks Rosemary Villanucci because she must "assert her pride;" it is this feeling that also causes her to attack the white dolls. When Pecola comes into the house, Claudia is concerned about her guest's feelings, and does her best to accommodate her. Pecola truly comes to life, however, when she sees the image of Shirley Temple on the cup. The symbol of a fantasy world stimulates Pecola. Claudia has seen this type of behavior before, and immediately realizes that Pecola, like so many others, is enamored with movies and the white actresses that star in these movies.

Morrison's contrast between fantasy and reality is used to establish two themes that will run throughout the novel. The first is beauty, and how this idea affects Claudia, Frieda, and Pecola. All of the adult characters seem to identify blond and blue-eyed white girls as "beautiful." Claudia always gets the pretty white dolls that her elders had wanted when they were children. Mr. Henry compliments the girls by calling them "Greta Garbo" and "Ginger Rogers", both white actresses. As a result, the young black girls in

this story will grow up feeling that they are ugly and inferior. Each girl deals with this inferiority differently. Claudia hates the dolls that she receives as gifts for birthdays and Christmas, which seem to be more valuable to grown-ups than Claudia herself is. So Claudia lashes out at these symbols, ripping out their eyes and tearing off their heads in an effort to find out "what it was that all the world said was lovable." She also hates Shirley Temple, because she dances with Bojangles in a famous movie scene when that man "ought to have been soft-shoeing it and chuckling with me." She resents these white girls who have the love of both black and white adults, because they steal the attention and love that Claudia deserves.

Pecola and Frieda, however, are both enamored by these white girls themselves. Pecola is enraptured with the Shirley Temple cup, and drinks three quarts of milk just so she can hold the cup. Pecola is introduced as someone who is outdoors, which is someone without a home, and consequently, no one to count on. While Claudia presents her own parents with love, she already has contempt for Pecola's father because he is guilty of putting his family outdoors. Pecola's father has apparently failed to give his daughter the protection that she needed, and as a result, Pecola is terribly insecure. Claudia and Frieda try hard to be her friends, but they clearly have a long way to go in order to give Pecola a sense of security. Pecola seems to find this security only by drinking milk from the Shirley Temple cup.

The second theme introduced in this chapter is the theme of injustice. Claudia, Frieda, and Pecola are at the mercy of adults, who deal out whippings and beatings without concerning themselves with the reasons for punishment. Claudia feels that "adults do not talk to us—they give us directions." The theme of injustice is connected to the idea of beauty as well. It seems that the "ugly" Pecola, Claudia, and Frieda are always victims of injustice. Pecola begins to menstruate at Claudia and Frieda's house, and Mama whips Frieda when she catches them trying to clean Pecola in the backyard. They are punished for "playing nasty," even though menstruation is a natural process. The symbols of prettiness, such as the cup and the dolls, are not real, yet the adults treat these symbols as if they were. Pecola and Frieda are punished for being "nasty" because they are not able to be the same as the dolls, that

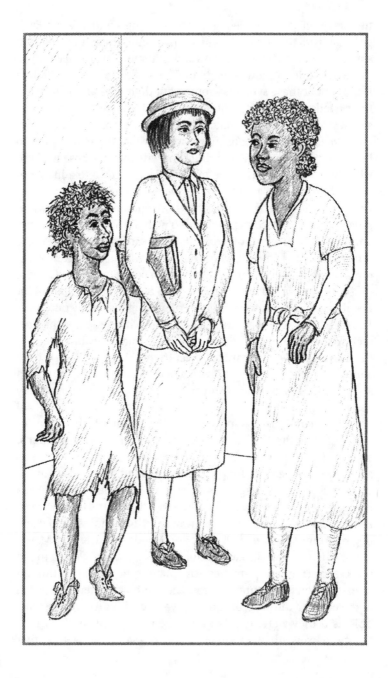

is, clean and plastic. The fact that no girl, white or black, could possess this fake beauty makes the punishment all the more unfair and cruel.

It seems that the allure of this fantasy world has had a profound effect on Pecola's character. Even though the reader has just been introduced to her, Pecola is presented as extremely passive, especially when shown alongside the doll-crushing Claudia. Pecola quietly accepts her fate, even when presented with injustice. She doesn't resist when Claudia's mother prepares to spank her, and Claudia must quickly come to her defense. Their response to the injustice of being beaten suggests that Pecola is used to being hurt. Another aspect of Pecola's character that immediately comes to attention is her immaturity. Even though Pecola should be "grown-up-like," she is in fact ignorant of what she must do to have a baby. She possesses the responsibilities of a woman but still resorts to asking Frieda what one must do in order to have a baby. The fact that Pecola is not aware of the facts of life makes it easy for the reader to forget that she is in fact "a little-girl-gone-to-woman." Pecola and Claudia's reactions to different situations should be noted while reading this novel.

Study Questions

1. Why do Claudia and Frieda beat up Rosemary, and what does Rosemary offer as an apology?

2. What does Claudia do once she falls ill?

3. How does Claudia describe Mr. Henry when she first meets him?

4. What game does Mr. Henry play with Claudia and Frieda when he first sees them?

5. What does Frieda and Claudia's Mama mean when she says that a "case" is coming to live with them?

6. According to Claudia, what is the difference between being put out and being put outdoors?

7. Where is the rest of the Breedlove family while Pecola is at Claudia's house?

8. Why does Mama complain about "folks" when she knows that Pecola drank three quarts of milk?

9. Why does Frieda ask Claudia to bring "lots of water?"

10. What does Claudia think will happen when she hears water running in the bathtub?

Answers

1. Rosemary asks the girls if they want to humiliate her by taking down her pants, and the girls show how strong they are by refusing to do so.

2. Claudia lies in bed while Frieda blocks the window with stockings. Claudia lies completely still in order to stay in the spot that she has made warm. After about an hour, her mother comes in and rubs salve on her chest. After she makes Claudia swallow a bit of the salve, her mother than wraps her in a flannel and puts a heavy quilt on top of her.

3. Claudia describes Mr. Henry almost entirely by his scent, which is "like trees and lemon vanishing cream, and Nu Nile Hair Oil and flecks of Sen-Sen."

4. Mr. Henry hides a penny on his body for Claudia and Frieda to find.

5. The "case" is a girl who is homeless and is now set up in the care of the county because her father committed arson. The county decides to place the girl in the care of Claudia's parents while her father is still in jail.

6. If you are put out, at least you may still go to another place, while being put outdoors is a final condition. Claudia says that this is "like the difference between the concept of death and being, in fact, dead."

7. Pecola's father, Cholly, is in jail while her mother is staying with the family she worked for as a maid. Pecola's brother, Sammy, is with another family.

8. Mama "never named anybody" when she complained about the behavior of a child, but these "soliloquies" were still said within earshot of the intended victim.

9. Frieda wants water so that she could clean off the steps, where Pecola's blood has left a stain.

10. Claudia is afraid that her mama will drown Pecola.

Suggested Essay Topics

1. Is Claudia fond of her mother? Does the mother's actions in this chapter make her a sympathetic character? Why or why not?

2. What sort of role does shame play in the lives of these girls?

Chapter 2
(Hereisthehouseitisgreenandwhite...)
and Chapter 3
(Hereisthefamilymotherfather...)

New Characters:

Mrs. Breedlove (Pauline): *Pecola's mother; works as a housekeeper for a rich white family and has a crippled foot*

Cholly (Charlie) Breedlove: *Pecola's father; a terrible drunk who fights often with his wife*

Sammy Breedlove: *Pecola's older brother*

China, Poland, and Miss Marie: *three prostitutes who live in the apartment above the Breedlove family*

Mr. Yacobowski: *the owner of a local grocery store*

Summary

The reader is told about the history of the house in which the Breedloves live. It is not a rich or interesting history. In fact, so many people have come and gone that it is hard to remember who has lived there before the Breedloves move in. The family's furniture is also unimportant and uninteresting, providing only use without the joy and comfort that some people receive from their furniture. The Breedloves have no happy memories, and live their lives with the unspoken belief that they are all ugly.

One morning in October, Mrs. Breedlove wakes up, and begins to wake up Cholly so that he might get some coal from the house. Cholly came home late the night before, drunk, and Mrs. Breedlove is looking for an excuse to start a fight with him, a fight that they couldn't have the previous night because Cholly was so drunk. Cholly is unable to get up, and Mrs. Breedlove leaves to get coal, warning him that she had better not sneeze while she is up. Of course, Mrs. Breedlove sneezes once, and throws a pan full of cold water on Cholly's face. While Cholly and his wife are fighting, Pecola is hiding underneath her blanket, trying once again to make herself disappear.

Pecola can never make herself completely disappear. No matter how hard she tries, she can always feel the presence of her eyes. She believes that if she had blue eyes, everyone would treat her nicely. Instead, other children either tease or ignore her, while adults simply ignore her. She blames the abuse she receives on her own appearance and prays every day for blue eyes. One day she goes into a store to buy candy, and feels uncomfortable when Mr. Yacobowski, the store owner, doesn't pay any attention to her. He stares at her, but it is a stare without any recognition, "because for him there is nothing to see." Pecola feels humiliated as she asks for the Mary Jane candies. When she walks out of the store, she can sense anger and shame well up inside her. Tears come into her eyes, but she is able to stop crying by eating the Mary Jane candies and looking at the white girl on the wrapper. She sees the "smiling white face" and the "blue eyes looking at her out of a world of clean comfort." This gives Pecola the desire to "be Mary Jane."

After buying the candies, Pecola visits the prostitutes that live upstairs. Poland, China, and Miss Marie are the only people in the town that treat her kindly, so Pecola often stops in to see them. The women love to entertain the child with stories about their former loves and the places that they have seen. Miss Marie tells Pecola about a boyfriend that she once had, a man whom she had loved before she found out she could make money as a prostitute. After hearing Miss Marie's stories, Pecola wonders once again about what love means between two people. If Pecola's parents fight, does that mean that she must fight as well in order to find love? She tries to picture her parents in bed together but cannot. As the girls laugh and sing with each other, Pecola wonders if the girls "were real."

Analysis

The first chapter of the novel was narrated by Claudia. While first-person narration is effective in terms of drama, this type of narration can only present the events from the point of view of one character. In the next two chapters, the events are told from the point of view of an omniscient narrator, a narrator that can see everything. This type of narration allows the reader to see events that Claudia could never see, such as Pecola's troubles in the candy store. An omniscient narrator may also mention the thoughts of a character, something which a first-person narrator would have no way of knowing.

As a result of this new narration, these chapters provide more insight into the Breedlove family, and Pecola Breedlove in particular. The reader learns that the Breedloves are a family in name only. The Breedloves are simply a group of individuals, each one primarily concerned with their own feelings. When they do interact with one another, it is with cruelty. Unlike the MacTeers, however, who are sometimes unfair to each other but do show love, the Breedloves inflict pain upon each other without remorse. It does not seem as if this family could act towards each other in a different way.

The one characteristic that seems to connect the Breedloves to each other is ugliness. Everyone in the Breedlove family looks and feels ugly, and this directly affects their self-esteem. While they are poor, "their poverty…was not unique." They live in a storefront that no one else would live in "because they believed they were ugly." Since the Breedloves do not offer support or love to each other, each member is left with his or her own ugliness, "dealing with it each according to his way." The way each Breedlove deals with this ugliness gives the reader insight into their character. Mrs. Breedlove uses her ugliness for "support of a role she frequently imagined was hers—martyrdom." Cholly and Sammy use their ugliness as an excuse to lash out at others. Pecola, however, does not use it as an excuse for self-pity as the others in the family. She desperately wants to be beautiful, and escape the cruel curse of her ugliness.

Mrs. Breedlove, on the other hand, needs to be perceived as ugly to complete her identity as a woman who must work her whole life away for a good-for-nothing husband. She can't wait to start a fight with Cholly, and the reader gets the idea that she was going to sneeze even before she warns Cholly about it. Cholly and Mrs. Breedlove fight because they need to fight each other. For Mrs. Breedlove, fighting represents "all the zest and reasonableness of life." Because she believes herself to be a woman who shows the proper respect for God, she needs Cholly so that she can compare herself to a true sinner. If Cholly ever managed to stop drinking and turn his life around, Mrs. Breedlove "...would never have forgiven Jesus." She needs her husband so that she can be a more successful martyr. Martyrdom has replaced motherhood in Mrs. Breedlove's life. The fact that her own children call her "Mrs. Breedlove" indicates that she has not been successful as a mother. When Mrs. Breedlove wants Cholly to get some coal, she repeatedly mentions how cold she is, but never points out how the children must be suffering. After she has had her fight, she turns to Sammy and orders him out of bed for the coal. Mrs. Breedlove finds it very easy to ignore the children when her desires have been fulfilled.

Pecola had decided long ago that the reason she did not receive love and support from her family was that she herself was ugly. Pecola connects the themes of injustice and beauty by her prayers for blue eyes. She feels that once she has blue eyes, the world will look upon her with love and respect. Until that time, she must put up with the abuse of her peers. She has put up with this abuse all her life, and now she expects it. One important scene that illustrates her passivity is in the candy store. The owner refuses to acknowledge her and Pecola cannot speak up for herself. She knows that the owner regards her with distaste, but Pecola finds the fault in "her [own] blackness," and blames herself for the shame that she feels. She is able to buy her candy, but as she walks away, she is ashamed of herself and her eyes tear up. She manages to keep herself from crying, however, by remembering the Mary Jane candies. The Mary Jane candies that she eats in this chapter once again represent her desire for blue eyes and white skin. Just as she drank milk in order to be near to Shirley Temple, her desire for candy represents her desire for the symbol, not the actual sweets. The narrator remarks that "to eat the candy is somehow to eat the eyes;" Pecola feels a brief connection to beauty when she possesses the symbols

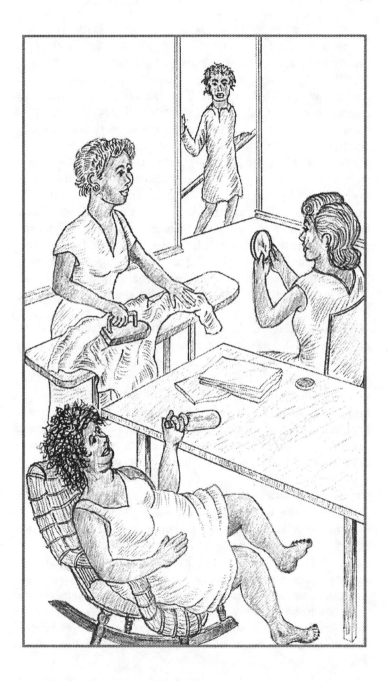

of beauty. However, Pecola uses these symbols to hide from reality as well. If Pecola had allowed herself to cry, she might have felt shame and have been provoked to defend herself. Instead, she takes refuge in these empty symbols of beauty, and withdraws into her fantasy world. She would rather "disappear" than confront the poverty that she lives in and the hatred that she receives from others. She is willing to be a victim if she can still have her candies, her milk, and feel close to these beautiful symbols.

While Pecola seems to be the victim of her own ugliness, she does have friends in the three prostitutes who live upstairs. These women are considered beautiful not by their appearance but by their actions. Pecola is in awe of them because they freely love whomever they want and live in their own way. The fact that the town and society considers their behavior low does not bother them in the least. Although Pecola listens to their stories, she can never believe that she could live life in the same way. Pecola is looking for society's acceptance, because she falsely believes that this could make her happy. She doesn't even see that Poland, China, and Miss Marie are as happy as they could be without society's acceptance. The text in this section is adoring of the three prostitutes; Miss Marie even belches "lovingly." They shower affection upon Pecola, but this does not seem to be enough for her. Ironically, Pecola wonders if the prostitutes are real; it never occurs to her to question Mary Jane or Shirley Temple, unreal symbols of the fantasy world in which she lives. While the three black women live out their fantasies, Pecola is not convinced that this is a way that she could live. The narrator states that "if Pecola her intention to live her life as [Poland, China, and Miss Marie] did, they would not have tried to dissuade her or voiced any alarm." While the narrator does not mean to suggest that Pecola should be a prostitute, the three women do prove that a happy, full, free life can be had without blue eyes and blond hair. However, Pecola cannot be convinced that the women are "real," so she will once again go back to her fantasy world. Pecola would rather have the Mary Jane candies than the reality of life. It never occurs to her to find happiness without blue eyes.

Study Questions

1. What is the history of the Breedloves' home?

2. Why is the fact that "the furniture had aged without becoming familiar" significant?

3. What was "the only living thing" in the Breedloves' house, and what does this phrase mean?

4. Why do the Breedloves live and stay in the house?

5. Why does Pecola hide beneath the sheets when Mrs. Breedlove wakes up?

6. What does Sammy say to Mrs. Breedlove as she fights Cholly?

7. How does Cholly fight Mrs. Breedlove?

8. How does Pecola make herself disappear?

9. Why is it so difficult for Mr. Yacobowski to notice Pecola, according to the narrator?

10. What is unusual about Miss Marie's pet names for Pecola?

Answers

1. The building is now an abandoned store. There used to be a pizza parlor there, which replaced a real estate agency. Before the real estate agency, a family of gypsies lived there. But even before gypsies lived there, that store was occupied by the Breedloves.

2. A house is usually the scene of many significant events in the life of a family. The narrator mentions some typical instances of family life, such as a child losing a penny in the sofa, a drunk person playing a piano at a party, or a little girl decorating a Christmas tree. While most of us can look at an item in our home and remember something pleasant, no such memories exist in the Breedlove home. Since the Breedloves have no happy memories, it can be inferred that they have spent little time together as a family, loving and supporting each other.

3. "The only living thing" in the house is the coal stove, which means that it is the only thing in the house that changes its behavior and lives independently of others.

4. The Breedloves "lived there because they were poor and black, and they stayed there because they believed they were ugly."

5. Pecola understands that Mrs. Breedlove is getting up in order to start a fight with Cholly, and hides in order to shield herself from the unpleasant scene.

6. Sammy yells, "Kill him! Kill him!"

7. Cholly fights her in the same way "a coward fights a man— with feet, the palms of his hands, and teeth." It is implied that Cholly understands why Mrs. Breedlove needs to fight him, and that Cholly has decided not to hurt her as badly as he could because of this understanding.

8. She hides underneath her blanket, closes her eyes, and parts of her body begin to vanish. She has to lie very still in order for the bigger parts of her body, such as her stomach, to disappear. But try as she might, she can never make her eyes disappear.

9. The narrator wonders "how can a 52-year-old white immigrant storekeeper with the taste of potatoes and beer in his mouth" notice a little black girl since "nothing in his life even suggested that the feat was possible."

10. Miss Marie's pet names for Pecola are all connected with food. Miss Marie refers to Pecola as "dumplin'," "chittlin'," "puddin'," "sweetnin'," and "chicken."

Suggested Essay Topics

1. Is there a piece of furniture or article of clothing that you especially like because of its connection with a special event in your life? What is this special event, and what role did this item play in that event?

2. "Mrs. Breedlove was not interested in Christ the Redeemer, but rather Christ the Judge." Explain what is meant by this sentence.

3. Explain the use of dandelions as a symbol in this chapter.

WINTER
Chapter 4

New Characters:

Maureen Peal: *a new girl in school who immediately becomes very popular*

Bay Boy, Woodrow Cain, Buddy Wilson, and Junie Bug: *four boys who are teasing Pecola in the playground*

Summary

Maureen Peal, a new girl in Claudia and Frieda's school, becomes popular because she is rich and light-skinned. Claudia tries to concoct a plan to humiliate her, but to her dismay, she discovers that everyone loves Maureen and wishes to become her friend. One day Maureen starts a conversation with Claudia, who holds the locker next to hers. When Maureen decides to walk home with Frieda and Claudia, Frieda is delighted but Claudia is still wary of her. As the girls head across the playground, they spot Pecola Breedlove, who is being teased by a group of boys. Frieda quickly rushes in and rescues her from the boys. Maureen begins to talk with Pecola, and they seem to get along really well. Maureen spots a drugstore up ahead and asks the girls if they want to have an ice cream. Claudia and Frieda decide that they like Maureen but are shocked when it becomes apparent that Maureen is going to treat only Pecola to ice cream. Ashamed because they expected to be treated to ice cream as well, Claudia and Frieda stay outside the drugstore.

The conversation turns to the facts of life, and Maureen asks Pecola if she has ever seen a naked man. Pecola replies defensively that she would never look at her naked father, but Maureen wants to know why Pecola mentioned her father. Seeing Pecola so uncomfortable, Claudia and Frieda jump at the chance to tease Maureen. Claudia swings at Maureen but hits Pecola instead. Frustrated by her inability to hit Maureen, Claudia begins to chase her and yells "You think you so cute!" Maureen escapes, yelling back at them, "I *am* cute! And you ugly!…I *am* cute!" Claudia and Frieda quickly return the insults but Pecola stares at the ground, apparently upset that Maureen has left. Claudia is frustrated at Pecola

for refusing to fight for herself, yet she admits to herself that Maureen Peal's words were painful because "if [Maureen] was cute...then we were not."

Claudia and Frieda walk home and find Mr. Henry alone in a bathrobe. Mr. Henry gives them a quarter to buy some ice cream. The girls, however, are still upset from their fight with Maureen Peal and do not want to return to the scene of the fight so quickly. They decide to buy candy at the local drugstore instead. Coming home, they see Mr. Henry laughing with China and Miss Marie, whom they call the Maginot Line. When Frieda asks him why the women were with him, he jokes with them but also asks them not to tell their parents. Frieda and Claudia are scared of the prostitutes, especially the Maginot Line, whom their mother "wouldn't let eat out of one of her plates." They decide not to tell their mother about them because the Maginot Line did not actually eat anything off of a plate in the house.

Analysis

Maureen Peal embodies white society's ideal of beauty, and provides a contrast in character to the miserable Pecola. At the chapter's beginning, Maureen, even though she has just entered school, has already become the most popular girl in the school. It is her unique appearance which makes her so popular. She is as rich as the "richest of the white girls," with long brown hair and green eyes. As an outsider, Claudia and Frieda expect to have some fun at Maureen's expense, but are shocked and disappointed when their peers immediately embrace Maureen. This makes Claudia jealous, and she spends her days trying to find some flaw or imperfection that she can use as a way to tease Maureen. Claudia has to be satisfied with making fun of Maureen's name because she cannot find anything ugly about Maureen. Although Claudia dislikes these beautiful girls, she has been brought up to believe that these girls were beautiful, and cannot find a weakness within this beauty.

It is not so hard for the children to find ways to tease Pecola. When Claudia, Frieda, and Maureen leave the school, they find a circle of boys around Pecola. The boys have created a chant that makes fun of the fact that Pecola has dark skin and the gossip that her father sleeps in the nude. It doesn't matter that the boys have the same tone of skin as Pecola; the narrator points out that "it was their contempt for their own blackness that gave the...insult its teeth." The boys are able to transfer this self-hatred upon Pecola, who readily accepts it because she already believes that she is ugly. Pecola's low self-esteem makes her easy prey for the boys who wish to bring up her supposed ugly appearance while forgetting that they share many of the same physical characteristics.

The children in this chapter feel shame rather easily and are always quick to defend themselves against this shame. When Maureen asks Claudia and Frieda if they intend to buy ice cream, Frieda quickly answers no. They were expecting Maureen to pay for them and do not want to be caught in their mistake. Pecola is ashamed when Maureen asks her if she has ever seen a naked man, and Claudia and Frieda quickly defend Pecola in order to release the anger they have for being poor.

Claudia and Frieda like themselves and usually don't mind not having money, but Maureen Peal's money, beauty, and popularity are too much for them to take. It doesn't satisfy them to think of names for Maureen, because even if they do tease her or defeat her in a fight, she will still be more popular than they ever will. Claudia compares her fight with Maureen with the destruction of the dolls. Destroying the symbol of beauty will not destroy their parents love of beauty. Claudia understands that "dolls we can destroy, but we could not destroy the honey voices of parents and adults...when they encountered the Maureen Peals of the world." This is what ultimately frustrates Claudia and Frieda in their struggle with Maureen.

What is just as frustrating is the fact that Pecola seems to side with Maureen in this quarrel. Maureen is not as cruel as the boys who tease her, but begins to make her feel uncomfortable when she asks her about her father. However, when Claudia and Frieda chase her away, Pecola still stares at Maureen as if she were wishing that Maureen would return. Although she was shamed by Maureen, she still had a few moments when she could forget she was ugly. Having a beautiful little girl for a friend made Pecola feel beautiful as well. It was the closest that Pecola had come to having blue eyes herself. Maureen compares Pecola to a "mulatto" character in a movie called *Imitation of Life*. Pecola is overjoyed to be identified with a character in a movie, and a light-skinned character no less. This identification gives Pecola reason to believe that her wish might finally be coming true. (Incidentally, the character's name in *Imitation of Life* was actually *Peola*, not Pecola.)

So the loss of this "friendship" is more distressing to Pecola than being teased by Maureen. She does not even thank Claudia and Frieda for coming to her defense, even if they were defending themselves as well. Claudia cannot understand this and is angered at the shame that Pecola feels. Claudia wants "to ram a stick down that hunched and curving spine" in order to "force her to stand erect." While the insults hurt Claudia, she is at least used to fighting in her defense and standing up for herself. Pecola once again displays her passive character, and shows that she will hide in the symbols of society's ideal of beauty when faced with a challenge. Claudia's fight with Maureen was an opportunity for Claudia to assert her character, while Pecola sees this fight as a lost opportunity to become someone else.

Morrison has already established the contrast between Claudia and Pecola, and reinforces this contrast through their interaction with Maureen Peal. Pecola envies Maureen and wishes to become her friend, while Claudia sees the injustice in Maureen's popularity. Maureen is a doll in flesh and blood, and like the plastic dolls, is undeservedly loved by adults and children. Claudia is able to lash out at Maureen, just as she hurt the dolls, but the fact that she misses Maureen and hits Pecola reinforces the theme of injustice in this novel. Pecola certainly did not deserve to be hit, but this has been happening to her throughout her life. The "beautiful" Maureen will be able to go through life unscathed, while Pecola is unable to avoid the blows and cruelty of others.

Study Questions

1. Why does Maureen start a conversation with Claudia?
2. How does Frieda break up the circle of boys teasing Pecola?
3. Why do the boys stop teasing Pecola?
4. Why do Claudia and Frieda begin to like Maureen?

5. What was Claudia thinking about before it became clear that Maureen was not going to treat her to ice cream?

6. Why does Maureen tell Pecola not to eat the end of the cone?

7. Why do boys have belly-buttons, according to Maureen?

8. Why doesn't Frieda want to go to Isaley's?

9. How does Henry explain Poland's and the Maginot Line's visit?

10. What does Frieda know about Woodrow Cain that she threatens to tell everybody?

Answers

1. Maureen happens to have her school locker next to Claudia's.

2. Frieda breaks into the circle by hitting Woodrow Cain over the head with her school books.

3. The boys stop teasing Pecola when they see Maureen in the distance. The boys are attracted to Maureen and do not want to be seen as bullies when she is watching.

4. Frieda and Claudia are surprised that Maureen would be so friendly to Pecola, and are pleased by her behavior. They are also still excited about their victory in the fight with the four boys.

5. When Claudia realizes that Maureen is not going to treat her, she attempts to conceal the fact that she "fully expected Maureen to buy [her and her sister] some ice cream, that for the past 120 seconds [she] had been selecting the flavor, that [she] had begun to like Maureen, and that neither [Claudia nor Frieda] had a penny."

6. Maureen thinks that there could be a fly hiding in the tip of an ice cream cone.

7. Maureen isn't sure why boys have belly buttons, but merely says that "boys have all sorts of things they don't need."

8. Frieda is afraid that Maureen could be sitting there.

9. Henry tells Claudia and Frieda that the prostitutes were "some members of [his] Bible class." He was supposedly "reading scriptures" with them.

10. Frieda heard that Woodrow Cain has a bed-wetting problem.

Suggested Essay Topics

1. Could Pecola and Maureen have maintained a friendship if Claudia and Frieda had not argued with Maureen?

2. How does the children's discovery of Mr. Henry with the prostitutes change their perception of him?

3. Claudia hates Maureen Peal and wishes to destroy her. Pecola wishes to become Maureen Peal. What is Frieda's reaction to Maureen Peal? Compare and contrast her behavior with Maureen to Claudia's and Pecola's behavior.

Chapter 5 (Seethecatitgoesmeow...)

New Characters:

Louis Junior: *a light-skinned black boy who invites Pecola back to his house*

Geraldine: *Louis Junior's mother*

Summary

There is a type of woman who lives in Lorain but comes from one of the bigger cities of America. This type of woman has dedicated her life to her own appearance, her education, and her family life. She has lived hoping that she will marry so that she may possess a house and a yard. Once she is married, she will become the head of the household and preserve this title at the expense of her own family. This type of woman has devoted her life to removing any sort of "Funk," whether it be dirt, disorder, or sex. She would have sex with her husband, but it was always an inconvenience. She always made sure that her hair was as straight as possible, and her skin as smooth and pale as possible. One such woman, named Geraldine, moved into the town of Lorain.

One thing was able to provoke love out of Geraldine: her cat. She had a son, Louis Junior, and she made sure that he was warm and clean. She also kept his hair straight and his skin pale. She did not, however, soothe and cuddle him; all her true affection was reserved for her cat. Louis Junior understood this, and grew up hating the cat. He would torture and abuse the cat any time that they were alone.

Louis Junior lived near the playground of Pecola's school. He didn't have many friends, because he was only allowed to play with the "colored children," as opposed to the "niggers." Because Louis lived so near the playground, he spent most of his time there asking, or forcing, children to play with him. However, if children didn't stay long enough to suit him, Junior would throw a rock or some gravel at them. As time passed, Junior "became a very good shot."

One day, Junior stops Pecola, who is taking a shortcut through the playground. He invites her to come into his house. Pecola doesn't want to stop in at first, but eventually is enticed by the promise of kittens. Once she gets in the house, however, Junior leads her into a room, throws the cat at her, then slams and holds the door behind her. Pecola, scratched and trapped, begins to cry. The cat comes up to her legs, and Pecola begins to pet it. Junior wonders why the crying has stopped, and enters the room to find the cat with the same look of content that it has when his mother, Geraldine, pets it. This causes Junior to lose control, and he seizes the cat and swings it around the room. Pecola tries to stop him, and in doing so, Junior lets go of the cat, which flies against the window. Geraldine comes home to find Junior and Pecola on the floor with the cat by the radiator. Junior quickly accuses Pecola of killing the cat. Geraldine moves toward the cat in sorrow, and looks at Pecola. Geraldine thinks of the time and effort she has put into herself to prevent being the type of woman that she sees in Pecola, and tells her to get out of the house. Pecola backs out of the house, while Geraldine cradles the cat in her arms.

Analysis

The idea of beauty has been presented almost strictly in terms of skin color. Shirley Temple and Mary Jane are sweet and beautiful, and have light skin. Pecola, who has dark skin and eyes, is "ugly."

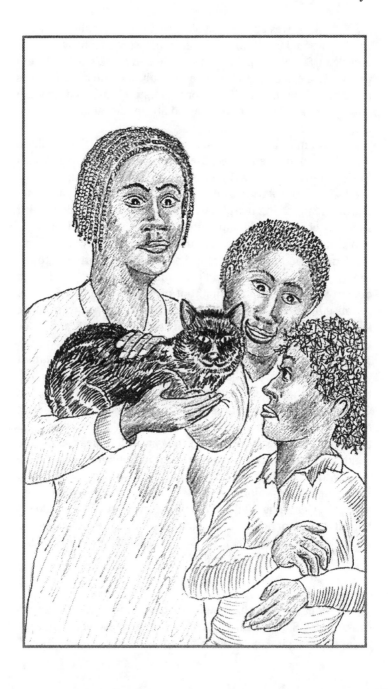

Pecola feels ugly because she believes that skin and eye color are directly related to beauty. However, the symbols of beauty that Pecola focuses upon do not actually exist. Shirley Temple hair will always be golden and her smile never vanishes because she is always seen within a film. Mary Jane's beautiful white skin is pressed onto a candy wrapper; the face will always look the same. The reason Pecola feels so ugly is that she compares herself to the unreal. Whether these symbols are actually beautiful or not, Pecola could never change herself to such a degree because as unfortunate as it might be, she lives in a real world.

In the previous chapter, Maureen Peal demonstrated the problems of trying to live up to such an ideal of beauty. Her light skin and green eyes might come close to white society's ideal of a pretty girl, but it is impossible for her to mimic Shirley Temple all of the time. When Claudia is not impressed by her beauty, Maureen is quick to lash out at her with cruelty. This exposes Maureen for what she is, a cruel little girl that has sacrificed her humanity for exterior beauty. However, no matter how beautiful Maureen is, she will always be nothing more than a spoiled brat. Even though Maureen thinks she is cute, and society might even agree with her, she will never be able to completely become a Shirley Temple or a plastic doll. Her exterior beauty will attract attention and love, but Maureen will always be dissatisfied as long as a girl like Claudia is not impressed. For the first time, the reader is presented with the negative side of this "beauty."

Geraldine is a different light-skinned woman, but she may as well be Maureen Peal as an adult. Geraldine and Louis Junior have the same physical characteristics as the other dolls and near-dolls, but it can hardly be said that these are beautiful people.

Geraldine has sacrificed any pleasure she could have had for this "beauty." She, in fact, maintains this beauty because she is fixated with society's ideal of what makes a person beautiful. She associates beauty with skin color in much the same way as Pecola does, and therefore has learned to hate her own skin because she is not white. She is so full of self-loathing that she wants to eliminate any trace of her color, in favor of pale skin and straight hair. She also decides to eliminate what she considered to be the emotional characteristics of blacks, in an effort to change her color. In her mind, the elimination of blackness meant "the careful development of thrift, patience, high morals, and good manners" while getting rid of "passion,...nature,...[and] the wide range of human emotions." So she devotes her life to changing herself, and makes a "successful" transformation. She is now as pretty as a doll, and as soulless as one.

Geraldine's elimination of passion from her life also results in her not being able to give love to another human being. Her son suffers from her lack of love. Geraldine is only able to give her son physical comfort, and finds it impossible to "talk to him, coo to him [and] engage him in kissing bouts." Since she doesn't like to interact with other blacks, she also severely restricts her son's interaction with others. As a result of this lack of love from family and friends, Louis Junior becomes a sociopath, insisting that others play with him because he doesn't know how to be friendly. When he is refused, he responds with violence. Junior is frustrated because he sees Geraldine give love to the cat, yet he is somehow excluded from her affections. This resentment causes Junior to focus his attacks upon girls in the playground, but his plans are usually thwarted because the girls travel together and can defend themselves. This makes Junior all the more frustrated, so he sets out to find a victim that he can overcome.

He finds that victim in Pecola. When Pecola becomes Junior's target, she finds herself abused at the hands of the cat. Junior is satisfied because he is finally able to hurt the cat and a girl. However, Pecola overcomes her pain and begins to stroke the cat. The cat immediately responds, because he too is merely a victim of Junior's manipulations. When Junior does not hear Pecola's crying, he walks in and finds that his plan has backfired. Junior watches the pleasure on the cat's face, and snaps because "he had seen that expression many times as the animal responded to his mother's touch." He is upset because he has once again been denied pleasure because of the cat, and responds by smashing the cat against the window.

Geraldine, however, is too self-centered to understand that she is ultimately responsible for this. All that she can understand is that her source of pleasure has been destroyed and one of the "niggers" that she has devoted her whole life to avoiding is now in her house.

She takes out her anger on Pecola because she, like her own son, is too misguided to blame herself. She tried to distance herself from blacks because she could not stand being black herself. Like Junior, Geraldine lashes out at the easily seen symbols of ugliness. The theme of injustice is once again shown, because Geraldine and Junior have devoted their lives to their own hatred, their own "ugliness." Even though they believe themselves to be beautiful, they have both lived the ugliest of lives, and will continue to take out their bitterness and resentment on other blacks, long after Pecola leaves their house.

Study Questions

1. Why would a man want to marry a girl like Geraldine, according to the narrator?

2. Where would a woman like Geraldine want her own private parts to be, and why?

3. What does Geraldine smell like?

4. What did Geraldine forbid Junior to do?

5. Who did Junior play with?

6. What does Junior tell his parents when he is beaten up by a bunch of girls?

7. How do Junior's parents respond to his story?

8. Junior notices that no one ever plays with Pecola. What does he believe is the reason for this?

9. What is Pecola's first impression of Junior's house?

10. Geraldine looked at Pecola and decided that she "had seen this little girl all of her life." Explain what is meant by this phrase.

Answers

1. Men would always want to marry women like Geraldine because they would eat well and live in a clean house.

2. Geraldine would always wish that her private parts would be in a more convenient place, such as her armpit, so that her husband could have sex with her without her needing

to take down her dress. Since sex was always an inconvenience to her, she would want to get it over with as quickly as possible.

3.   Geraldine smells like wood and vanilla.

4.   Geraldine never allowed her son to cry.

5.   Junior would only play with Ralph Nisensky, who was two years younger than him and not much fun to be around.

6.   Junior tells his parents that he was beaten up by Bay Boy. Bay Boy was one of the boys that teased Pecola until Frieda rescued her.

7.   Geraldine was outraged, but Louis, the boy's father, did not even look up from his paper.

8.   Junior decides that no one ever plays with Pecola because she is ugly.

9.   Pecola is impressed by the beautiful house.

10. Pecola is the type of girl that Geraldine has hated all her life. She decides that she is going to grow up to have low morals and bad manners. Her parents are loud and obnoxious, and do not have the sense to take care of her. These children "clowned on the playgrounds, broke things in dime stores, [and] ran in front of you on the street." Geraldine had avoided this type of person all her life.

Suggested Essay Topics

1.   What do you believe the symbol of the statue of Jesus at the end of the chapter represents?

2.   What do you think Geraldine will do after kicking Pecola out of the house?

3.   Why do Pecola and the cat identify with each other so easily?

SPRING
Chapter 6

New Character:

The Fishers' daughter: *the adorable daughter of the family that has hired Mrs. Breedlove as a maid*

Summary
One spring Saturday, Claudia returns from playing outside and finds the house unusually quiet. She goes to her bedroom and finds Frieda crying on the bed. Frieda tells her sister that Mr. Henry had touched her breasts. When Frieda's father found out, he tried to shoot Mr. Henry but missed. Frieda cannot stop crying, and Claudia wonders if their mother had beat her. Frieda finally breaks down and tells Claudia that a neighbor told their parents that Frieda might be "ruined." Frieda is scared because she believes she will turn out like the prostitutes that their mother always talks about. Frieda is afraid that she will become fat, but Claudia remembers that China and Poland are "ruined" but thin. China and Poland drink whiskey, so the girls conclude that "ruined" people drink whiskey in order to stay thin. They decide that they need to get whiskey and head towards Pecola's house, since her father is a drunk.

When Frieda and Claudia get to Pecola's house, they find the Maginot Line sitting on the porch of their apartment drinking root beer. Both Frieda and Claudia are scared because they believe they "were seeing what was to become of Frieda." Claudia finally asks about Pecola's whereabouts, and she is told that Pecola is with her mother at the edge of town. Pecola's mother works as a maid for a white family, and Pecola is helping her with some chores. The Maginot Line invites them to come up and wait for Pecola but Frieda refuses, saying that they were told not to come near her. The Maginot Line simply laughs and throws the empty root beer bottle at the girls, narrowly missing them. The girls run away and decide to walk to the end of town.

They find Pecola by the house and Mrs. Breedlove calls them into the kitchen of the house. The three girls wait for Mrs. Breedlove to get the laundry. While they are waiting, a little white girl in a pink dress asks them where "Polly" is, and Claudia feels hatred

rising in her. Their thoughts, however, are diverted by a fresh berry cobbler on the windowsill. Pecola wants to touch it to see if it is still hot, but accidentally spills it on herself. Mrs. Breedlove quickly runs up and starts slapping Pecola for ruining the floor, and then consoles the little white girl, who is crying because the pie is ruined. She orders Pecola, Claudia and Frieda to clean up the mess and promises the little white girl that she will make another pie.

Analysis

This chapter can be easily divided into two halves in terms of action. The first half of the chapter chronicles Frieda's fear that she will be "ruined" and Claudia and Frieda's encounter with the Maginot Line. The second half of the chapter concerns Mrs. Breedlove's cruel punishment of Pecola for accidentally knocking over a pie. This chapter focuses upon two characters who have dual identities, the Maginot Line (also known as Miss Marie) and Mrs. Breedlove ("Polly"). In this chapter, the Maginot Line and Mrs. Breedlove both must react in situations where their double lives are revealed. Their reactions are important not only in the context of their characterization, but in the context of the novel's central themes.

Claudia and Frieda are scared of the Maginot Line when she is in fact one of the smarter and nicer women in the town. However, the only one who seems to know the sweet side of the Maginot Line is Pecola. This is implied by Pecola's use of the name "Miss Marie." Pecola doesn't even know whom Claudia and Frieda are talking about when they mention "the Maginot Line." Claudia and Frieda, meanwhile, cannot believe that Pecola is not scared of the Maginot Line, and ask Pecola if she has ever eaten out of their plates. Pecola seems to understand that the town doesn't like the women, but nevertheless defends the Maginot Line with simple logic; even though Pecola's mother doesn't like them, Pecola knows that the women are nice because "they give [her] stuff all the time." Pecola has met and talked with these women, and knows that they have good hearts.

Claudia and Frieda had never met the three women but have been taught to fear them by their parents. Frieda is scared she will become like these women, yet they never have known exactly why they should be afraid. So when Miss Marie offers them some soda, Claudia is ready to accept the gesture of kindness. Frieda, however, remembers that they are not allowed to visit and is still afraid that she will be "ruined." When Claudia and Frieda look at Miss Marie, they were both "seeing what was to become of Frieda." Actually, Miss Marie was kind and friendly until Frieda tells her that she is already "ruined." Miss Marie throws a soda bottle at the two children in response to their ignorance. The Maginot Line throws the bottle quickly, with "a gesture so quick and small" that is hardly seen by the girls. This is the response Miss Marie will always have for those who do not agree with her lifestyle. She is so full of confidence and love that she does not feel the need to convince anyone about her character. Miss Marie is generous and kind to those that appreciate her company, such as Pecola. She controls the world in which she lives, and is not so easily influenced by the opinions of others.

Mrs. Breedlove, by contrast, is content to be the maid of a family at the edge of town. She spends her life pleasing and taking care of others. When Claudia and Frieda come into the house at the edge of town, they find Pecola and Mrs. Breedlove in a beautiful clean kitchen where the smells of cooking food hover in the air. This house is a dream when compared to the squalid little storefront in which Mrs. Breedlove's own family lives. Mrs. Breedlove not only has devoted her energy to the upkeep of this white family, but also has treated this family with much more affection than she had shown her own family in the second chapter.

This point is emphasized by the presence of the little white girl in a Shirley Temple outfit. When Claudia sees the white girl, she can feel her familiar anger, but it is the familiarity with which the girl addresses Mrs. Breedlove that really upsets Claudia. The girl's reference to Mrs. Breedlove as "Polly" seems to Claudia enough "reason to scratch her." The fact that the girl is able to address Mrs. Breedlove in a way that even her own daughter cannot seems immediately unfair to Claudia. The ultimate contempt, however, falls upon Mrs. Breedlove for betraying her own daughter. Mrs. Breedlove is not only able to ignore Pecola's pain when she knocks over a hot pie, but also beats her own daughter for upsetting the pretty little girl. Mrs. Breedlove cannot forgive Pecola for the disruption that she has caused, and forgets her own daughter in favor of the little girl. It seems terrible that Mrs. Breedlove can show love for a complete stranger and either ignore or abuse her own daughter. This treatment reinforces Pecola's idea that people would treat her differently if she had blue eyes. As for Mrs. Breedlove, she seems to have given up the poverty of her own family in favor of a new identity. She is more than happy to be "Polly," and resents her own daughter for intruding upon that identity.

Study Questions

1. Why is Claudia jealous of Frieda?
2. What is Claudia's initial reaction to the news about Mr. Henry?
3. What does being "ruined" mean to Frieda?
4. What happens when Miss Dunion suggests that Frieda should be taken to a doctor?
5. What is a "Maginot Line?"
6. Why do Frieda and Claudia go to the second-story porch?
7. How does Claudia react to Pecola's smile when they meet at the house by the lake?
8. Where is Pecola going to go with Poland and China?
9. What is Mrs. Breedlove wearing while she works?
10. Describe what the little girl is wearing.

Answers

1. Claudia complains that her chest is much smaller than Frieda's.
2. Claudia is jealous for a number of reasons. She is upset about having to hear the big news from Frieda, and complains that she "always misses stuff." She also considers Frieda to be lucky to have been pinched by Mr. Henry, since she is so flat-chested she has "nothing to pinch."

3. Frieda thinks that being "ruined" means that she will become "like the Maginot Line." As the image comes to Frieda's mind, they decide that being ruined means that Frieda will become fat.

4. Frieda's mother begins to yell at Miss Dunion for suggesting that her daughter might be ruined.

5. The Maginot Line was the name of an elaborate blockade by soldiers along the border of France during World War II. The Maginot Line was intended to stop an invasion of France by Germany, but the Germans were able to bypass the French defenses.

6. The girls hear loud music playing from upstairs and decide to see if Pecola is upstairs.

7. Claudia becomes happy when she sees Pecola's smile. She had not realized that she had rarely seen Pecola smile, and "is surprised at the pleasure" that she receives from this smile.

8. Pecola claims that China is going to take her to Cleveland, while Poland is going to take her to Chicago.

9. Mrs. Breedlove is wearing a white uniform.

10. The little girl is dressed in a pink dress with pink bunny slippers. Her hair is blond and braided.

Suggested Essay Topics

1. Compare and contrast the characters of Mrs. Breedlove and Mrs. MacTeer (Claudia and Frieda's mother).

2. What sort of relationship does Mrs. Breedlove have with the little white girl in the pink dress? Can you compare this with any other relationship previously shown or mentioned in the novel?

3. What is the significance of Miss Marie's nickname?

Chapter 7
(Seemothermotherisverynice...)

New Characters:

Ada and Fowler Williams: *Pauline Breedlove's parents*

Chicken and Pie Williams: *Pauline's younger twin brothers*

Ivy: *a singer in Pauline's childhood church*

The Fishers: *the family that hires Mrs. Breedlove as a maid*

Summary

Ever since Pauline Williams was a child, she felt inadequate because of her crippled foot. A childhood injury left her with a deformity and means of identification, but she felt that no one paid her attention. She was the only child in her large family that did not have a nickname, no one told anecdotes about her, and she had "a general feeling of separateness and unworthiness." She felt something was missing from her life, and that the reason it was missing was her broken foot.

She spent her time cleaning and taking care of the other children in the house. When the other children were old enough to work and leave the house, Pauline, who enjoyed cleaning and cooking, then started to take care of other people's homes. The one thing that Pauline wanted at this time was a sense of order, and she was able to find this order in cleaning. One day, while sitting on a fence, she was cleaning her nails when she felt something tickling her foot. She looked down, laughing, into the eyes of Cholly Breedlove. Cholly's gesture gives Pauline the feeling that she is beautiful; "for the first time, Pauline felt that her bad foot was an asset." Cholly is able to affect Pauline "just as she had dreamed," and give her the security that she had longed for.

Cholly and Pauline were married, and moved up north to Lorain, Ohio. Unfortunately, their marriage started to fall apart. Pauline felt uncomfortable with her clothes and took a job in order to buy new clothes. Cholly was unhappy with these purchases and began to spend more time drinking. Soon they would begin to quarrel, and these vicious quarrels turned into fights. The marriage

deteriorated to a point where Pauline spends most of her time at the movies. Things became better when Pauline was pregnant, but then she lost one of her front teeth eating a candy bar, and when Cholly laughed about it, Pauline tried to kill him.

After Sammy was born, Pauline tried to have another baby quickly, and told herself she would "...love it no matter what it looked like." But when Pecola was born, Pauline "...knowed it was ugly." Pauline realized that she was too old to believe that life could be like in the movies and was fortunate enough to find work with the Fishers. In her job, she was able to be close enough to the life she had wanted. She still thinks about leaving Cholly, but she can remember the few moments of passion they had had together, and cannot bring herself to leave. Whatever happens in the future, Pauline knows that "my Maker will take care of me. I know He will."

Analysis

This chapter is devoted to an extended character study of Pauline Breedlove. Reading about her, we find out that she is a much more sympathetic character than in previous chapters because she, like Pecola, had dreams and desires that were destroyed by her marriage to Cholly and her own "ugliness." However, like the other characters in this novel, she eventually transfers her own inadequacies and faults onto Pecola, and blames her own family for her problems.

The narration in *The Bluest Eye* has switched from first-person to omniscient several times, depending upon which sort of perspective was necessary. This chapter introduces an entirely new narrative system. A traditional omniscient narrator, which presents events in an unbiased fashion, and Pauline herself (the text in italics) tell the story in this chapter. Therefore, this chapter has the feel of a magazine article; the omniscient narrator's comments and observations are presented with occasional comments from the "subject," Mrs. Breedlove.

The previous chapter, written from Claudia's perspective, portrayed Mrs. Breedlove as a woman who had "adopted" a little white girl in place of her own daughter. This chapter allows Pauline to present her own motivation for keeping her job and private life separated. Although Pauline still seems cruel for abandoning her

family, the reader may understand that this cruelty may have been necessary for her own preservation. The reader now sees that Pauline has been a victim of injustice herself, especially in her relationship with Cholly.

Like Pecola, Pauline becomes obsessed with society's symbols of beauty. Her marriage with Cholly falls apart because Cholly responds to their poverty by drinking and staying away from Pauline. Pauline herself admits that "the onliest time I be happy seem like was when I was in the picture show." While watching the actresses on the screen, Pauline becomes obsessed with the idea of physical beauty, which the omniscient narrator calls "probably the most destructive idea in the history of human thought." Pauline desperately tries to imitate the hairstyles of the actresses in order to become beautiful. However, she gives up trying to emulate these actresses when she loses a tooth. This loss of beauty is too much for Pauline, and she admits that she was never able to overcome it. Even with beautiful hair, the loss of a pretty smile dooms her, in her mind, to a life of ugliness.

This is why she enjoys working at the Fishers' place. Even though she is still ugly, she is still surrounded by the trappings of success and beauty. This happy life comes only when she reduces her fantasies and learns to be satisfied with a subsidiary role. She used to imitate the hairstyles of Jean Harlow, but her role is now that of a housekeeper, not unlike the roles that black actors and actress were limited to in the movies of the time. Nevertheless, she is able to have "beauty, order, cleanliness and praise" at the Fishers' home, which is something that her own family has apparently never given her. The Fishers appreciate her and their little daughter calls her "Polly;" this familiarity and respect is what Pauline has always wanted. Because she receives so much pleasure from this work, and it is the closest she will ever come to her fantasy life, she does not share this life with others. Sammy and Pecola only remind her of her own less than perfect life, so she does her best to exclude them from her work. When they do enter her work, they only intrude upon her fantasies (by spilling her berry cobbler, for example).

As a result, she devotes her efforts to the Fishers, which results in more rewards, and deprives her own family of a strong maternal figure. Since "all the meaningfulness of her life was in her work,"

she undermines her own effectiveness as a mother to her own children. Nevertheless, she believes that she is "fulfilling a mother's role" when she punishes the children for "any slovenliness, no matter how slight." She doesn't realize that by hitting Pecola, she has given her daughter "a fear of growing up, fear of other people, fear of life." Her neglect of Pecola is not intentional, but is a result of her retreat into a fantasy world.

Morrison illustrates the destructive power of fantasy through the character of Pauline. Pauline's decisions have been based upon moments of ecstasy; she runs away with Cholly because she is able to feel beautiful with him for a short period of time. Even though their marriage has deteriorated, she still focuses upon the times when they made love, and "it be rainbow all inside." She admits that "it ain't like that anymore," but still cannot let go of her fantasies. The omniscient narrator of this chapter warns that "to find out the truth of about how dreams die, one should never take the word of the dreamer." The passages in Pauline's words show that she has put her fantasies ahead of her real life, and that these fantasies now sustain her while she walks through her real life.

Study Questions

1. How many brothers and sisters did Pauline have?
2. What fantasies kept her from doing her work?
3. How does Pauline feel when Cholly tickles her?
4. How does Pauline's happiness with Cholly compare with her fantasies?
5. What becomes the focus of their quarrels?
6. How is Pauline surprised by Cholly when she tells him she is pregnant?
7. What does the doctor say about Pauline and black women in general?
8. Name the groups and organizations of which Pauline is a member.
9. What would Mr. Fisher rather do than sell real estate?
10. Where is the "meaningfulness" in Pauline's life?

Answers

1. Pauline had ten brothers and sisters; she was the ninth of eleven children.

2. "Fantasies about men and love and touching" were distracting her from her work.

3. When Cholly tickles her foot, Pauline feels all of the pleasant memories of her youth and the colors she associates with these memories. The yellow from the lemonade she drank, the purple of the berries she picked, and the green of the grass "all come together…inside [her]."

4. Pauline feels the happiness of her fantasies "minus the gloom of setting suns and lonely river banks." There was always a streak of melancholy in her fantasies because she was isolated and alone. Once she meets Cholly, she understands what it truly feels like to be in love.

5. Money becomes the focus of their quarrels. Pauline needs money to buy clothes, while Cholly needs money to get drunk.

6. Cholly is pleased when he finds out that she is pregnant.

7. The doctor says that "these here women" deliver with no pain, "just like horses."

8. In addition to being an active member of the local church, Pauline is a member of the Stewardess Board No. 3 and Ladies Circle No. 1.

9. Mr. Fisher would rather sell Pauline's berry cobblers than real estate.

10. Pauline has found significance and "meaningfulness" in her work.

Suggested Essay Topics

1. Having read about Pauline's dreams and the effect that these dreams have had upon her life, what can be said about Pecola's use of fantasy and the effect this fantasy will probably have upon *her* life?

2. Rewrite a scene in an earlier chapter from another character's point of view. (For example, how would Maureen Peal have told the story about her fight with Claudia and Frieda?)

Chapter 8 (Seefatherheisbigandstrong...)

New Characters:

Aunt Jimmy: *the aunt of Cholly's mother, who had abandoned Cholly right after he was born; raised Cholly herself*

Blue Jack: *an old man who worked at the feed store with Cholly; he used to entertain Cholly with stories*

M'Dear: *a respected midwife who also prescribed home remedies for the ladies of the town*

O. V.: *Aunt Jimmy's brother*

Jake: *an older cousin who tries to pick up girls with Cholly*

Darlene: *Cholly's first girlfriend*

Samson Fuller: *Cholly's father*

Summary

Cholly was raised by Jimmy, his great aunt. His mother had left him by a railroad track, and when Aunt Jimmy found out about it, she beat Cholly's mother (her own niece) and took the baby away from her. Aunt Jimmy named Cholly after her own brother, rather than his father, because "ain't no Samson [Fuller] ever come to no good end." Cholly had a pleasant childhood and fondly remembered Blue Jack, a man who used to tell him stories while he worked in a feed store. Blue Jack became a father figure to Cholly, which was something that Cholly would appreciate later in life.

Aunt Jimmy died while Cholly was a young adolescent. At the funeral, Cholly meets one of his distant cousins, a fifteen-year-old named Jake. Jake and Cholly decide to look for some girls while the reception is going on, and Cholly meets a young girl named Darlene. Darlene and Cholly go off into the woods and talk with each other. The talking soon turns to kissing, and the two young

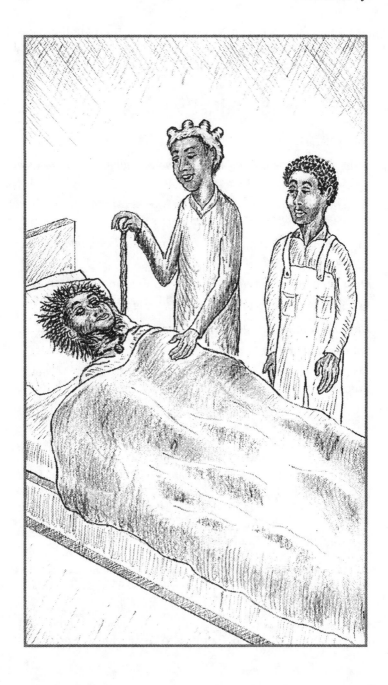

lovers begin to undress each other. However, two white hunters find them in the grass, and as Cholly begins to pull up his pants, one of the hunters points his gun at him, and orders Cholly to continue, adding that Cholly had better "make it good." Cholly is unable to do anything because of fear, so he fakes having sex with Darlene, at the same time hating the girl for seeing him like this. The hunters get bored and leave, and Cholly and Darlene also walk home in the rain.

After the incident, Cholly is afraid that Darlene will become pregnant. He cannot even tell Blue Jack about his problems; he feels that the only person who might understand is his real father, since he had also made a girl pregnant and abandoned her. He decides to travel to Macon and find Samson Fuller. After walking from town to town, he finally is far enough away from home to travel without fear, and takes the next bus to Macon. He finds his father playing craps in an alley, but when he goes up to introduce himself, he realizes that he does not know his mother's name. Samson Fuller, mistaking him for a messenger sent by another girlfriend, tells him to go away. Cholly walks away and sits down on a sidewalk trying not to cry. He manages not to cry, but in doing so soils his trousers. As he goes down to the river to wash himself, he realizes how much he misses Aunt Jimmy, and cries into the night.

The next morning, however, he begins a new life in which he need only worry about himself, since his parents are no longer a concern. He leads a dangerous and happy life, full of drunken adventures. Until he meets Pauline Williams, Cholly lives totally for himself. However, once the children come, Cholly is bewildered. Since he had no actual parents, and even those who had loved him left him at an early age, he cannot know how to raise children himself. This makes him feel uncomfortable whenever the children are around, because he is unable to "comprehend what such a relationship should be" between parents and their children.

One day, Cholly comes home drunk and finds his daughter washing dishes. He hates himself because he cannot give anything to his daughter, and he hates Pecola because she looks like a whipped girl, who is weak-willed. He is about to be sick when he notices that Pecola is scratching one leg with the bare foot of the other leg. It reminds him of when he first met Pauline. When

Pauline did it, Cholly wanted to scratch away the itch himself. He does it once again with Pecola. Pecola is surprised by the way her father touches her and falls on the floor. Cholly catches his daughter and rapes her on the kitchen floor, which causes Pecola to faint.

Analysis

Cholly's biography serves the same sort of purpose that Pauline's biography had served; the chapter provides the reader with motivation for Cholly's actions. This is very necessary in light of Cholly's rape of Pecola at the end of the chapter. It is very easy to condemn the rape as a horrible, meaningless act, but to do so would also render the novel meaningless. Understanding why he does it is important to understanding *The Bluest Eye*.

Cholly was also a victim of injustice; he is forced to have sex with a girl at gunpoint. The shame and humiliation that he feels is turned into hatred for the girl, Darlene. He never considers being angry at the white men who forced him to have sex; he seems to know subconsciously that "such an emotion would have destroyed him," the frustration and inability to exact revenge. He hates Darlene because she is "the one who had bore witness to his failure,...the one whom he had not been able to protect." Because he cannot tell anyone about this, not even his friend Blue Jack, his suppressed rage will become his motivation for later actions. He tries to find his father because he thinks that Samson Fuller, a man who could not take care of a woman he impregnated, might be able to understand his feelings of impotence and rage. When Fuller rejects him, however, he is forced to take care of himself.

Cholly's desire to protect and destroy affects his future relationships with women. He is enamored by Pauline because with her broken foot she seems like a person easy to protect. However, the relationship soon deteriorates because it becomes clear to Cholly that he has not been able to take care of his wife. Full of self-pity, Cholly tries to avoid his wife and drink so that he may forget that he has not provided for his wife. The situation becomes worse when he and Pauline have children. Since he has no idea how to raise children, he leaves them alone, which only adds to his feelings of shame and impotence. His impotence is exacerbated by Pecola's nature as well. Seeing her wash the dishes with a

hunched back causes Cholly to become upset. He wonders what has happened to Pecola to make her so miserable, and takes this personally. "The clear statement of her misery was an accusation" to Cholly, an accusation that he had not protected her as a father should have protected his daughter. He transfers the shame that he feels for not protecting his daughter into hatred for his daughter, just as he did with Darlene when he couldn't protect her.

Yet when he sees Pecola hunched over washing the dishes, he is also touched by her. Even though her weakness and shame parallels his vision of Darlene being ashamed for him, he still has this desire to comfort and protect her with his love. The problem for Cholly is that he has no idea how to love his daughter. He wants to do something "tenderly" to his daughter. However, his two desires are to "break her neck—tenderly" and to "fuck her—tenderly". He is limited to these two choices because he doesn't know how to protect a person any other way. His first experience with Darlene has warped his judgment, and has caused him to associate sex with feelings of shame and inadequacy. The only time he has successfully conquered these feelings is when he caressed Pauline's leg and tickled her foot. So when Pecola scratches her leg, Cholly is finally moved into attempting an act of protection, not even caring that this is a completely inappropriate response to his own shame. The rape is not an act of cruelty in his eyes, but the only way he knows how to take care of a woman. The fact that Pecola is not just a woman but his own daughter does not enter his mind until the action is completed.

While the action itself is possible to explain, the fact that Cholly runs away from his responsibility ultimately proves that he is unable to take care of others. Just as he left Darlene to her fate, Cholly cannot accept the consequences of his own actions now. When he is plagued with shame, he performs acts that he feels will redeem his past behavior but actually only cause him to feel more shame. His rape of his own daughter was the ultimate act, the most misguided attempt to correct his past behavior. After doing this, Cholly escapes, proving that he has not been able to rid himself of his self-pity.

Study Questions

1. How does Aunt Jimmy supposedly die?

2. What are the future plans for Cholly after Aunt Jimmy's death?

3. How does Cholly embarrass himself asking for a cigarette?

4. Why does Cholly miss Aunt Jimmy when he goes into the field with Darlene?

5. Why doesn't Cholly live with his uncle, O. V.?

6. How does "a Georgia black boy" run away?

7. Why does the man at the bus window sell Cholly an under-twelve bus ticket even though he is certain Cholly is lying about his age?

8. What makes Cholly cry thinking about Aunt Jimmy?

9. Why is Cholly's sequence of emotions "revulsion, guilt, pity, then love" when he sees Pecola washing dishes?

10. What does Pecola see when she regains consciousness?

Answers

1. Aunt Jimmy was told by M'Dear, the local midwife, to drink nothing but pot liquor, but one of her friends unwittingly brings her a peach cobbler. Aunt Jimmy eats a piece and dies soon after.

2. Cholly will move in with Aunt Jimmy's brother, O. V., and his family.

3. He tries to light the cigarette without putting it in his mouth first.

4. Cholly realized that if Jimmy were alive, she would beat him for going off to play after dark. Cholly misses her because there is no one to punish him if he does something wrong.

5. If Darlene is pregnant, Cholly is afraid of living in a town close to the town where Darlene lives. He thinks O. V. will make him marry Darlene if she is pregnant.

6. He walks from town to town and sleeps in an abandoned barn or haystack. Once he is far away enough, he can make some money doing jobs for a week at a time before moving to the next town.

7. The man decides to sell Cholly a children's ticket just in case Cholly is telling the truth about having no money and a sick mother in Macon.

8. Cholly remembers how Aunt Jimmy would give him a piece of ham for dinner, and pass the plate to him with no words but a tenderness that only a mother could have for their child.

9. Cholly is first repulsed because Pecola, hunched over washing dishes with dirty water, is a pitiful figure. Cholly then feels guilt because he believes that it is his own inadequacy as a father which has caused his daughter to be miserable. He then feels sorry for Pecola because she is miserable. Finally, Cholly wants to protect Pecola and make her feel safe, so his pity turns to love.

10. When Pecola wakes up after the rape, she sees her mother looking over her, wrapping her in a quilt on the kitchen floor.

Suggested Essay Topics

1. Compose a dialogue between Samuel Fuller and Cholly Breedlove in which Cholly tells him that he is his son.

2. How does Aunt Jimmy compare in character to the other women in *The Bluest Eye*? Pick another female character and compare her to Aunt Jimmy.

Chapter 9
(Seethedogbowwowgoesthedog...)

New Characters:

Soaphead Church (Elihue Whitcomb): *a child molester who works as a 'spiritual guide' for the people of Lorain*

Velma: *Elihue's wife for a brief period of time*

Summary

Elihue Whitcomb was a person who always seemed to prefer the company of objects rather than people. However, his dislike for others could only mean that he would be in a profession that serves others. Although he briefly considered becoming a priest, he decided against it, instead choosing to be an analyst and interpreter of dreams. He enjoyed his job immensely, because he could witness the silliness of his fellow human beings every day. He believed himself to be superior to those that came into his office seeking advice, and seeing their weaknesses and humility merely fed his ego.

Elihue's personality was neatly ordered and well-balanced except for one flaw: his "rare but keen sexual cravings." His passions are directed towards little girls because they "were usually manageable and frequently seductive." The bodies of little girls lacked "all the natural excretions and protections the body was capable of," which disturbed his love of precision and cleanliness. Since he also hated physical contact, even the seduction of a girl "smacked of innocence and was associated in his mind with cleanliness." Ever since he had been abandoned by his wife, Velma, he had devoted his life to the elimination of filth and disorder. This desire for little girls reconciled his sexual desires with his obsession of cleanliness.

Elihue finally settled in Lorain, where the residents nicknamed him Soaphead Church. Since he had spent most of his life as a professional scholar, he could not find work easily, and went through a number of jobs. He finally became a counselor, a job he was well-suited for because he understood the psychology of human beings and could grant his clients relief from their sufferings simply by telling them what they wanted to hear. His clients "asked for the simplest of things," and Soaphead Church was always able to grant these requests because he never judged his clients for being greedy or destructive.

He rented an apartment in the house of an old religious lady, and enjoyed this arrangement, except for the old dog that slept by the entrance to his apartment. Soaphead Church's love of order and cleanliness was challenged every time he saw the dog at his front door. He had bought some poison to put the dog out of his misery. However, even being near the dog disgusted him, and he could not bring himself to finish the job.

Pecola Breedlove enters his office one day, with "a little protruding pot of tummy." She thinks that he can help her; she "can't go to school no more" and hopes that he can "do it for her." She asks him to give her blue eyes. To Soaphead Church, this is the most reasonable request he could ever hope to encounter. For the first time in his life, he wishes he could actually help people instead of manipulating their weaknesses. This wish then turns into anger, for he knows that he is a fake, and that there is nothing he can do to make Pecola's wish come true. As he looks toward his window, his eyes fall upon the dog, and he is inspired by an idea. He tells Pecola that he is merely an "instrument" of God, and she must perform a ritual in order to find out if God will grant her wish. He quickly retrieves the poison he bought and pours it over some meat, instructing Pecola to give the meat to the dog. If the dog changes his expression, God has heard her. The dog eats the meat and almost immediately convulses and dies. Pecola, shocked, runs away.

After this is all done, Soaphead Church takes out some paper and writes a letter to God. He curses God for giving him a life where people did not love him and a preference for little girls. Because of this, he has been forced to live his life as a misanthrope and sexual deviant. He also wonders why it was necessary for God to create a world in which Soaphead Church's only love could have abandoned him, a world in which little girls "sit on road shoulders, crying next to their dead mothers." Soaphead Church comes to the conclusion that God has "forgot how to be God." This is why he gave Pecola the blue eyes she wanted. He is proud of himself because he has done what God couldn't do. Even though only she will see those blue eyes, he has given Pecola happiness. After Soaphead Church finishes his letter, he folds it together and drifts off to sleep.

Analysis

It is easy to dismiss Soaphead Church because he is a charlatan and a child molester. Strange as it seems, this character has the most impact upon Pecola. Morrison uses him to illustrate the problems of faith and Pecola's reliance upon faith. By praying and going to this fake in hope of blue eyes, Pecola has resisted self-reliance and withdraws more deeply into the idea of being beautiful.

The rape has clearly destroyed Pecola. She is visibly pregnant when she enters Soaphead Church's office and says that she is no longer going to school. She has been abandoned by society, and this has caused her to take action against her shame, something which she had never done before. Unfortunately, her course of action is to ask for blue eyes, which is certainly nonsense in the context of her situation. Blue eyes wouldn't make her any less pregnant, but Pecola's solution to her personal problems has always been to hide in the symbols of beauty. Usually she internalizes her pain by eating a Mary Jane candy or praying for blue eyes. This time, under the pressure of being abandoned, she has turned away from God in hope of making her wish come true.

Soaphead Church was successful because he understood the nature of his clients. The clients that come to his door are regular citizens of Lorain, yet their desires are usually either self-serving or designed to harm others. This illustrates the base nature of the society in which we live. Soaphead Church attributes his success to his ability to grant requests without passing judgment on his clients. However, because the ones that come to his door lack the spirituality need to confront difficult situations, Soaphead Church now believes that the world is inherently base and evil. He decides that "evil existed because God had created it."

Yet when Pecola comes to his door asking for blue eyes, Soaphead Church is touched because this is the first request that he feels is necessary to grant. "Here was an ugly little girl asking for beauty," rather than for a material possession. Soaphead Church's bitterness toward God increases because, in his sense of order, God should have already granted this wish. Instead, Soaphead believes that God has brought this little girl to him in order to show him that he is a fraud. Soaphead believes he can turn the tables by tricking Pecola into believing that she has blue eyes. As he explains in his letter to God, he does "what You did not, could not, would not do," and believes that in doing this, he has created the miracle that God should have created, the miracle of making a little girl happy.

However, Soaphead Church's law of creation has a logical flaw. He does not have a high opinion of God's work because he likes the idea of order without the idea of balance. Although he does think that everything should be arranged and logical, this idea is not universally applied by Soaphead, especially the idea that good must exist alongside evil in order to maintain balance. He thinks that God's biggest fault was "creating an imperfect universe." It is beyond Soaphead's view to think that the universe must exist this way. Both Soaphead and Pecola believed that a supernatural force could alter the destiny of people living on Earth, while characters such as Claudia have shown that human beings are ultimately responsible for their own behavior. Soaphead Church never thinks that God does not grant wishes because it is unfair to take away the responsibility that humans must have for themselves.

So, Soaphead Church gives Pecola blue eyes in order to create something based upon his law of creation, rather than God's ideal. However, the fact that only Pecola will notice her blue eyes simply shows what false faith can do. Pecola is easily deluded because she had prayed to God for so long, only not to be answered. Instead of finding the answer within herself, Pecola turns to a second-rate god, who is only happy to oblige her. They both have succeeded in deluding themselves, but this will not make Pecola's eyes look different.

Study Questions

1. What is a "misanthrope?"

2. What is the significance of Soaphead Church's name?

3. What is the one thing that disgusts him more than touching a woman?

4. What does Pecola's request for blue eyes do to him?

5. Why does Evil exist, according to Soaphead Church?

6. What is meant when it is written that Soaphead Church's business "is dread?"

7. How does Soaphead Church address God in his letter?

8. What does Soaphead Church mean when he writes that Velma left him "the way people leave a motel room?"

9. To what does Soaphead Church compare the breasts of little girls?

10. What parts of sex does Soaphead Church avoid by molesting little girls, as written in his letter?

Answers

1. A misanthrope is a person who has a general hatred for other people.

2. He is called "Soaphead" because he uses soap bubbles as a hair pomade. No one is sure why "Church" became his last name, but it is suggested that a town resident had heard about his brief study in the ministry.

3. That one thing was touching and being touched by another man.

4. For the first time, Soaphead Church wishes that he could perform miracles.

5. Evil exists because it was created by God.

6. The people that come to Soaphead Church's office look for the power of God but do not understand that God's power comes from love. His clients want a supernatural force to help and protect their own interests. So they "came to him in dread, whispered in dread, wept and pleaded in dread" because they ultimately knew that what they wished for was horrible.

7. He writes his letter "TO HE WHO GREATLY ENNOBLED HUMAN NATURE BY CREATING IT."

8. When Velma left him, it was without regret or memory. A hotel room merely serves a temporary purpose, and once that purpose is fulfilled, the room is abandoned without a second thought. This is what he felt like when Velma left, as if he would no longer be remembered.

9. Soaphead Church compares the breasts of little girls to "not quite unripe strawberries."

10. Soaphead Church claims that when he has sex with little girls, it is done without the "nastiness," "filth," "odor," and "groaning" that accompanies sex between two adults.

Suggested Essay Topics

1. How would you respond to Soaphead Church's letter? Point out the flaws in his arguments.

2. Examine the events in Soaphead Church's life and how each event might have influenced his later behavior.

SUMMER
Chapters 10 and 11
(Looklookherecomesafriend...)

Summary

Claudia and Frieda are delighted to receive the packages of seeds that they had been waiting for all spring. They hope to sell enough seeds to earn a bicycle, so they begin to knock on the doors of their neighbors. They begin to pick up some gossip, and eventually realize that Pecola is pregnant by Cholly. They are hurt and ashamed for their friend, but they are hurt even more when they find out that no one seems to care about Pecola, and everyone hopes that the baby will be stillborn. Frieda and Claudia decide that they must want the baby to live in order "to counteract the universal love of white baby dolls, Shirley Temples, and Maureen Peals." They decide to say a prayer and sacrifice the seeds. They will bury the seeds and if the seeds blossom, they will know that Pecola's baby will live.

The seeds do not blossom. Pecola's baby is born prematurely and dies. Cholly and Sammy leave, while Pecola and Mrs. Breedlove move into a little house on the edge of town. As the years pass, Pecola spends most of her days roaming the streets and the dump, the laughingstock of the entire town. The only thing she talks about now is her blue eyes, and she lives in fear that someone will have eyes that are "bluer" than hers. Claudia, now an adult, comments on how the people of Lorain used to make themselves feel better at Pecola's expense. Claudia used to blame herself for letting the seeds die in the ground, but she has come to the understanding that it "was the fault of the earth, the land, of our town." In a cruel world, some people manage to survive, but for Pecola, "it's much, much, much too late."

Analysis

The outcome of Pecola's life is tragic but not surprising.
Morrison provokes controversy by having one of the women dis-
cussing Pecola claim that "she ought to carry some of the blame"
for being raped by Cholly. While that statement is outrageous, it is
also true that Pecola is not blameless for her descent into madness. Pecola has reacted to every injustice and attack by retreating
into a fantasy world of blue eyes and beauty. It is true that the pain
she felt at the hands of the other children was horrible. Maureen
Peal insulted her to feed her own ego. Louis Junior hurt Pecola out
of hatred for his own mother, and Geraldine was cruel to her out of
hatred of dark-skinned black people. Mrs. Breedlove ignored her
in order to live a life in her own fantasy world, and when Cholly
tries to give her the support that she had needed, he ends up rap-
ing her on the kitchen floor. All of this does not cause Pecola's
madness. Pecola goes insane because she had devoted her life to
obtaining that which she could never have. Her obsession with blue
eyes leads her to Soaphead Church, who deludes her into believing she has them. Rather than deal with the horrible things that
have happened to her, Pecola decides to retreat completely into
her fantasy world. It is not a fair choice for a twelve-year-old girl to
have to make, but it is still her choice.

Pecola walks around town with a mirror, looking at her own
eyes. When people look away from her, Pecola attributes these reactions to jealousy. Her actions are a grotesque parody of Maureen
Peal and what she imagines other beautiful girls must be like.
Pecola's imaginary friend is a manifestation of her madness; she
needs a friend in order to justify her delusion of blue eyes. This is
consistent with Pecola's idea that if she had blue eyes, she would
become popular. If she did not have new friends, then it would
mean that her eyes were not blue and Soaphead Church was a
fraud. So Pecola creates a new friend in her mind in order to keep
up the illusion that she has blue eyes. The conversation with her
friend shows that Pecola has completely detached herself from
reality. She refuses to acknowledge any of the previous events in
her life, even though her friend teases her with sly references to
Cholly and Maureen Peal. As much as Pecola represses these events,

they will still occasionally surface. Pecola will nevertheless find a way to keep these traumas hidden in her imaginary blue eyes.

Now that the novel has been read, the "Dick and Jane" passage at the beginning finally becomes clear. The structure of *The Bluest Eye* is parallel to "Dick and Jane"; each sentence from the passage introduces a new chapter in the novel. Elements from the passage are explored in each chapter; "Hereisthecat" features the cat used by Louis Junior to hurt Pecola, "Hereisthemother" is the chapter that focuses upon Mrs. Breedlove, and "Hereisafriend" introduces Pecola's imaginary friend, the friend that will finally play with her. Morrison uses this parallel development to show how far removed fantasy is from reality, and to paint a cold, cruel world in which children cannot simply play with others. Every person and object from "Dick and Jane" is cruel to Pecola in *The Bluest Eye*. It is not a surprise that Pecola would choose to hide in a world of fantasy.

The only person who understands why the people of Lorain are so cruel is Claudia. Claudia realizes that those that hurt Pecola were looking for a distraction from their own shortcomings. Claudia mentions how every member of Lorain is able to make themselves feel better at Pecola's expense:

> "All of us—all who knew [Pecola]—felt so wholesome after we cleaned ourselves on her. We were so beautiful when we stood astride her ugliness. Her simplicity decorated us, her guilt sanctified us, her pain made us glow with health, her awkwardness made us think we had a sense of humor....And she let us, thereby deserving our contempt."

Claudia mentions near the novel's end that "the soil is bad for certain kinds of flowers." The earth becomes a symbol for the environment in which Claudia, Frieda, and Pecola were forced to live. Claudia is angered at the fact that she had to be strong in order to survive her childhood. The injustice that the children have had to live with throughout their lives is a burden that no child should endure. While it is implied that the town had contempt for Pecola because she was weak, the sad truth is that society put this crushing responsibility on her in the first place. Pecola searched for blue eyes because she could not deal with this responsibility on her own terms. She is guilty of weakness, but this weakness should not have

led to insanity. She was forced to be responsible for herself, but society had left her unable to take care of herself. Claudia has discovered that "when the land kills of its own volition, we acquiesce and say the victim had no right to live?" Claudia survives because she was strong, while Pecola takes refuge under wishes and fantasies, a shelter that eventually collapses over her. In a more loving world, Pecola would never have wanted or needed blue eyes. *The Bluest Eye* has illustrated that a loving world cannot be counted upon. Claudia finally understands that "we are wrong" to place such a burden on children, but she doesn't care anymore, because she had only wanted to help Pecola, and it is "much, much, much too late" to save her.

Study Questions

1. What do Claudia and Frieda think about until they hear that Pecola is pregnant?

2. How long does it take for Claudia and Frieda to realize that Pecola is pregnant?

3. What type of "law" do the women say there should be against Cholly's actions?

4. What is Claudia's "only handicap?"

5. How long do the sisters promise to be good if God lets the baby live?

6. What reason does Pecola give for other people turning away from her?

7. How does Pecola's madness protect her from other people?

8. What did grown people do to Pecola after the baby was born?

9. What did children do to her?

10. Who loved Pecola?

Answers

1. Claudia and Frieda think about the money that they will make from the seeds and the bicycle that they would buy with the money. Because of this, it takes them longer to realize that Pecola is pregnant.

2. Claudia and Frieda realize that the pregnant girl is Pecola after half-listening to two or three conversations.

3. One woman says that there should be a law against "two ugly people doubling up...to make more ugly."

4. According to Claudia, size was the only reason that they could be picked on and bullied by others.

5. Claudia and Frieda promise to be good for an entire month.

6. Pecola thinks that other people turn away because they are jealous of her blue eyes.

7. The people of Lorain stopped making fun of Pecola because they became bored with her.

8. Grown people always looked away.

9. Children simply laughed at her.

10. In addition to the Maginot Line and Cholly Breedlove, it is clear from Claudia's words that she, too, had loved Pecola.

Suggested Essay Topics

1. Do you agree with Claudia when she says "Love is never any better than the lover?" Why or why not?

2. Do you think anything could have been done for Pecola, or was she doomed to become insane? Use examples from the text to support your position.

Sample Analytical Paper Topics

The following paper topics are designed to test your understanding of the novel as a whole and analyze important themes and literary devices. Following each question is a sample outline to help you get started.

Topic #1

Compare and contrast Claudia and Pecola in terms of their ability to fight injustice. How does this ability affect them later in the novel?

Outline

I. Thesis Statement: *Pecola and Claudia both live in a cruel world that does not allow innocence in children. Their survival in such a world depends upon their ability to fight injustice. Claudia is able to survive a cruel childhood because she never stops fighting. Pecola, on the other hand, retreats into a world of fantasy whenever she is attacked. Eventually, she must live her life in this world of fantasy because she can no longer passively defend herself from cruelty.*

II. Claudia aggressively fights for herself while Pecola is passive.

    A. Claudia stands up for herself.

        1. She gets revenge against Rosemary Villanucci.

    B. Pecola stands by while people abuse her.

      1.   She is teased by a circle of boys.

      2.   Louis Junior attacks her, then manipulates his mother into attacking her.

III. Claudia attempts to defend Pecola.

   A.   Claudia helps rescue Pecola from a group of boys in a playground.

   B.   When Maureen Peal insults Pecola, Claudia immediately responds.

IV. Cholly's rape of Pecola instigates her downfall.

   A.   She responds to the rape by asking Soaphead Church for blue eyes.

   B.   In her madness, she not only believes that she has blue eyes, she also tells her "friend" that Cholly "didn't do anything."

V. The people of Lorain force Pecola and Claudia to defend themselves or perish.

   A.   People feel that Pecola "ought to carry some of the blame" for Cholly's rape.

   B.   Claudia never let herself be bullied, while the townspeople have contempt for Pecola because she lets herself be pushed around.

   C.   In this town, "the soil was bad for certain kinds of flowers," and a frail flower such as Pecola could never survive.

Topic #2

Focus upon the characters of Maureen Peal and Geraldine. What characteristics do they share? Do these characters support Pecola's belief that pretty people have pretty lives?

Outline

I.   Thesis Statement: *Geraldine and Maureen Peal are considered beautiful by society but are unable to deal with others in personal relationships. The two characters develop a hatred of dark-skinned blacks because they consider themselves beautiful.*

II. Maureen Peal has learned that beauty is wonderful without sacrifice.

   A. She attains instant popularity at school.

   B. Pecola and others will do anything to be her friend.

   C. Maureen is aware of her own beauty and believes that she is special.

III. Geraldine has chosen beauty over passion in her life.

   A. She has resisted sexual relations and passion in favor of order.

   B. Her son brings her no joy.

   C. Because of her own beauty, she develops a hatred for "niggers" that masks her own self-loathing.

IV. Both Geraldine and Maureen Peal are unable to handle personal crises.

   A. Maureen Peal can only defend herself by calling others ugly.

      1. Her statement "I am cute! And you ugly!...Black and ugly!" indicates her awareness that people consider her beautiful because she is light-skinned.

   B. Geraldine reacts to the death of her beloved cat by blaming Pecola.

      1. Pecola's ugliness arouses hate in Geraldine.

      2. Geraldine believed that "she had seen this little girl all her life," and had devoted her life to distancing herself from girls like Pecola.

   C. When faced with a difficult situation, Geraldine and Maureen can only console themselves with their own beauty.

Topic #3

How do the light-skinned *male* characters reconcile their appearance with society's belief that blond, blue-eyed *girls* are beautiful? Focus upon Soaphead Church and Louis Junior in terms of their relationships with girls.

Outline

I.   Thesis Statement: *Louis Junior and Soaphead Church have a lot of anger directed towards women and girls, because they are unable to form relationships with other males.*

II. Louis Junior and Soaphead Church have no friendly relationships with other males.

    A. Junior is forbidden to play with other black boys, and eventually decides that he is too good for them.

    B. Soaphead Church considers boys to be "insulting, scary, and stubborn."

III. The lack of a father figure has an effect upon their lives.

    A. Junior

        1. Louis Senior was not interested in him, and he feels that lack of love.

    B. Soaphead Church

        1. He is beaten regularly by his father in an effort to instill discipline, which affects his relationship with his wife, Velma.

IV. The men feel hostility towards women as a result of their inability to form nurturing relationships.

    A. Junior

        1. Junior is bitter towards his own mother, even though he directs his hostility towards her cat.

        2. Junior enjoys teasing girls, even though he is overcome by a group of girls which only exacerbates his hostile nature.

    B. Soaphead Church

        1. Soaphead Church is unable to maintain a relationship with his wife.

V.   Reconciliation of their hostilities

    A. Junior finds a way to attack Pecola, his mother, and his mother's cat in a manipulative scheme.

    B.   Soaphead Church accepts his misanthropy and is no longer bitter towards God after he "helps" Pecola.

Topic #4

What part does shame play in *The Bluest Eye?* Look at major events in the novel and decide to what degree shame plays a part in making the characters act.

Outline

I.   Thesis Statement: *The characters in* The Bluest Eye *are motivated by shame to either defend themselves or lash out at those who are weaker.*

II.   Claudia is quick to defend any attacks on her pride.

    A.   She fights Rosemary Villanucci.

    B.   She shouts her "most powerful" insults at Maureen Peal.

        1.   Maureen Peal shames Claudia by not buying her ice cream.

III.   Cholly Breedlove is unable to defend himself, so he projects his anger on those he can defeat.

    A.   He must hate Darlene because he cannot attack the hunters who shame him.

    B.   His self-loathing plays a large part in his rape of Pecola.

IV.   Because Pecola has no shame, she becomes an easy victim.

    A.   She is shamed by Mr. Yacobowski, but decides not to cry.

        1.   The Mary Jane candies keep her from thinking about her shame.

    B.   She forgives Maureen for her insults but cannot thank Claudia for helping her when she is insulted by Maureen.

    C.   Even her own mother seems to reject her in favor of a pretty white girl, but Pecola simply regresses into a fantasy world.

SECTION FOUR

Bibliography

Morrison, Toni. *The Bluest Eye.* Pocket Books, New York, 1970.

Null, Gary. *Black Hollywood: The Black Performer in Motion Pictures.* Carol Publishing Group, New York, 1975.

Samuels, Wilfred D., and Hudson-Weems, Clenora. *Toni Morrison.* Twayne Publishers, Boston, 1990.

Toni Morrison: Critical Perspectives Past and Present, edited by Henry Louis Gates, Jr. and K. A. Appiah. Amistad Press, 1992.

The High School Tutors®

The **HIGH SCHOOL TUTOR** series is based on the same principle as the more comprehensive **PROBLEM SOLVERS**, but is specifically designed to meet the needs of high school students. REA has revised all the books in this series to include expanded review sections and new material. This makes the books even more effective in helping students to cope with these difficult high school subjects.

If you would like more information about any of these books,
complete the coupon below and return it to us or go to your local bookstore.

MAXnotes®

REA's Literature Study Guides

MAXnotes® are student-friendly. They offer a fresh look at masterpieces of literature, presented in a lively and interesting fashion. **MAXnotes®** offer the essentials of what you should know about the work, including outlines, explanations and discussions of the plot, character lists, analyses, and historical context. **MAXnotes®** are designed to help you think independently about literary works by raising various issues and thought-provoking ideas and questions. Written by literary experts who currently teach the subject, **MAXnotes®** enhance your understanding and enjoyment of the work.

Available **MAXnotes®** include the following:

Absalom, Absalom!
The Aeneid of Virgil
Animal Farm
Antony and Cleopatra
As I Lay Dying
As You Like It
The Autobiography of
    Malcolm X
The Awakening
Beloved
Beowulf
Billy Budd
The Bluest Eye, A Novel
Brave New World
The Canterbury Tales
The Catcher in the Rye
The Color Purple
The Crucible
Death in Venice
Death of a Salesman
Dickens Dictionary
The Divine Comedy I: Inferno
Dubliners
The Edible Woman
Emma
Euripides' Medea & Electra
Frankenstein
Gone with the Wind
The Grapes of Wrath
Great Expectations
The Great Gatsby
Gulliver's Travels
Handmaid's Tale
Hamlet
Hard Times
Heart of Darkness

Henry IV, Part I
Henry V
The House on Mango Street
Huckleberry Finn
I Know Why the Caged
    Bird Sings
The Iliad
Invisible Man
Jane Eyre
Jazz
The Joy Luck Club
Jude the Obscure
Julius Caesar
King Lear
Leaves of Grass
Les Misérables
Lord of the Flies
Macbeth
The Merchant of Venice
Metamorphoses of Ovid
Metamorphosis
Middlemarch
A Midsummer Night's Dream
Moby-Dick
Moll Flanders
Mrs. Dalloway
Much Ado About Nothing
Mules and Men
My Antonia
Native Son
1984
The Odyssey
Oedipus Trilogy
Of Mice and Men
On the Road

Othello
Paradise
Paradise Lost
A Passage to India
Plato's Republic
Portrait of a Lady
A Portrait of the Artist
    as a Young Man
Pride and Prejudice
A Raisin in the Sun
Richard II
Romeo and Juliet
The Scarlet Letter
Sir Gawain and the
    Green Knight
Slaughterhouse-Five
Song of Solomon
The Sound and the Fury
The Stranger
Sula
The Sun Also Rises
A Tale of Two Cities
The Taming of the Shrew
Tar Baby
The Tempest
Tess of the D'Urbervilles
Their Eyes Were Watching God
Things Fall Apart
To Kill a Mockingbird
To the Lighthouse
Twelfth Night
Uncle Tom's Cabin
Waiting for Godot
Wuthering Heights
Guide to Literary Terms
